THE CRAVEN COTTAGE ENCYCLOPEDIA

THE CRAVEN COTTAGE ENCYCLOPEDIA

An A–Z of Fulham FC

Dean Hayes

EDINBURGH AND LONDON

First published in Great Britain in 2000 by
MAINSTREAM PUBLISHING COMPANY (EDINBURGH) LTD
7 Albany Street
Edinburgh EH1 3UG

ISBN 1 84018 264 4

A catalogue record for this book is available from the British Library

Printed and bound in Great Britain by The Cromwell Press Ltd

ABANDONED MATCHES When Fulham visited Derby County's then Baseball Ground for the final match of the 1982–83 season, the Cottagers needed to win to gain promotion to the First Division whilst the Rams were fighting to avoid relegation. With just over two minutes to play, the home side were leading 1–0. Many of the 21,124 spectators had spilled over onto the touchline and, thinking mistakenly that the referee had blown the whistle for full-time, ran onto the pitch. The referee had no alternative but to take the teams off. Later, when it became apparent that it was impossible to restart the match, he admitted that he had abandoned the game. The Cottagers appealed to the Football Association to have the match replayed, but remarkably the game's authorities decided to allow the result to stand. Their reasons were twofold in that they felt Fulham wouldn't score twice in the two minutes of play that remained, and that it was nigh impossible to recreate the conditions of the last Saturday of the season when all promotion and relegation issues were settled.

ADAMS, MICKY Micky Adams started his footballing career as an apprentice with Gillingham and turned professional in 1979. After winning England Youth honours and appearing in 92 games for the Kent club, he was transferred to Coventry City in the summer of 1983 for £75,000. At Highfield Road, Adams was a virtual ever-present and scored nine goals in 90 league games before joining Leeds United in January 1987. After 73 league appearances for the Yorkshire club he was sold to Southampton for £250,000 and in five years at The Dell clocked up 174 first-team outings. After being given a free transfer, he had a brief spell at Stoke City before joining Fulham as player-coach in the

Micky Adams

summer of 1994. He made his début in a 2–1 defeat at Torquay United in September 1994, going on to end the season with 11 goals in 25 games. In February 1996 he was appointed the club's player-manager, at the time the league's youngest. Though injuries restricted his appearances in 1996–97, he led the club to their first promotion since 1982 in his first full season in charge and fully deserved his election as Third Division Manager of the Year. However, after scoring 12 goals in 35 games, Adams was allowed to leave Craven Cottage in October 1997 to take over the reins at Swansea. After just 13 days in charge of the club, but finding that money promised for new signings was not available, he walked out. He later managed Brentford, but in the summer of 1998 he left to become assistant manager at Nottingham Forest.

AGGREGATE SCORE Fulham's highest aggregate score in any competition came in the 1983–84 League Cup when they won both legs of the second-round tie against Doncaster Rovers 3–1. The 6–2 aggregate win saw the club's all-time leading goalscorer Gordon Davies score three of the goals. The Cottagers' worst aggregate score came in the same competition three seasons later when they were beaten 13–2 by Liverpool, including a 10–0 hammering at Anfield.

ANGLO-ITALIAN CUP When Swindon Town won the Football League Cup in 1969, they were ineligible for the Fairs Cup because they were not a First Division side. Consequently, they organised a match against the Italian League Cup winners, AS Roma, playing for the Anglo-Italian League Cup. The following year the Anglo-Italian Cup was introduced for club sides from the two countries who had no other involvement in Europe. Fulham entered the competition in 1972–73, drawing each of their three matches against Como (away 0–0), AS Roma (home 1–1) and Torino (away 1–1). The following season the Cottagers again drew their only match 1–1, at home to Bologna.

ANGLO-SCOTTISH CUP The Anglo-Scottish Cup was inaugurated in 1975–76 following the withdrawal of Texaco from sponsorship of the competition. Fulham were undefeated in their group matches, beating Norwich City (away 2–1) and Chelsea (home 1–0) and drawing 2–2 at Craven Cottage with Bristol City. In the quarter-final, the Cottagers beat Heart of Midlothian 5–4 on aggregate to set up a semi-final meeting with Motherwell. Despite being held to a 1–1 draw at Craven Cottage, Fulham won the away leg 3–2 to reach the first-ever Anglo-Scottish Cup final. After losing 1–0 to Middlesbrough at Ayresome Park, Fulham could manage only a goalless draw in the return leg at Craven Cottage and so had to be content as runners-up to the Teeside club. In 1976–77, the Cottagers failed to win any of their group games, losing 2–1 at Orient and drawing with Chelsea (away 0–0) and Norwich City (home 1–1). The following season, Fulham won all their group games against Orient, Chelsea and Norwich City by the same 1–0 scoreline but then lost 6–4 on aggregate to St Mirren in the quarter-final. In 1978–9, Fulham again failed to qualify for the knockout stages after losing 1–0 at Cardiff City and 3–0 at home to Bristol City and beating Bristol Rovers 2–1. It was a similar story for the next two seasons as Fulham beat Plymouth Argyle (home 1–0) but lost to Birmingham City (home 0–5) and Bristol City (away 0–1) in the 1979–80 group games and then to Bristol City (away 0–2) and Notts County (home 0–1) in 1980–81, although they did beat Orient (away 2–1) in their last-ever game in the competition.

APPEARANCES Johnny Haynes holds the record for the greatest number of appearances in a Fulham shirt with a total of 657 games between 1952 and 1970. Haynes played in 594 League games, 43 FA Cup games and 19 Football League Cup games.

The players with the highest number of appearances are:

	League	*FA Cup*	*FLgCup*	*Total*
Johnny Haynes	594	43	19	657
Eddie Lowe	473	33	5	511
Les Barrett	420(3)*	31(1)	36	487(4)
Frank Penn	428	32	–	460
George Cohen	408	33	18	459
John Marshall	393(18)	19(1)	33(1)	445(20)
Len Oliver	406	28	–	434
Jim Stannard	389	14	25	428
Les Strong	370(3)	28	26	424(3)
Arthur Reynolds	399	21	–	420
Albert Barrett	388	30	–	418

Gordon Davies	364(30)	28(1)	24(1)	416(32)

* figures in brackets indicate appearances as substitute

ARNOLD, JOHNNY Johnny Arnold began his football career with non-League Oxford City before moving to Southampton in 1929. He was at this time qualifying as a professional cricketer for Hampshire, but the following season underlined his potential as a goalscoring winger, netting seven times in 18 games. During the 1931–32 season he was the Saints' top scorer with 20 goals, netting in five consecutive games towards the end of the season. Midway through the following campaign he had scored 11 goals in 26 games including a hat-trick against West Ham United when, along with Mike Keeping, he was transferred to Fulham. His first game in Fulham colours saw him score the Cottagers' opening goal in a 3–3 home draw against Bury. Over the next six seasons, Arnold not only provided numerous goalscoring opportunities for players such as Jim Hammond, Eddie Perry and Ronnie Rooke, but scored his fair share too; 12 in 1936–37 being his best season. Arnold also helped Fulham reach the FA Cup semi-finals in 1935–36 and scored the Cottagers' goal in the 2–1 defeat by Sheffield United at Molineux. Within a month of his arrival at Craven Cottage, he had been capped by England in their match against Scotland. Arnold, who scored 63 goals in 213 games for Fulham, played until the outbreak of the Second World War. He continued to open the batting for Hampshire until 1950, scoring 21,596 runs. He appeared in one Test match for England, thus becoming one of the few men to represent his country at both sports. After his retirement from active sport, he became a first-class umpire, a position he held for twenty years.

ATTENDANCE – AVERAGE Fulham's average home League attendances for the past ten seasons have been as follows:

1989–90 4,484	1994–95 4,207
1990–91 4,057	1995–96 4,191
1991–92 4,492	1996–97 6,644
1992–93 4,736	1997–98 9,018
1993–94 4,655	1998–99 11,387

ATTENDANCE – HIGHEST The highest-ever attendance at Craven Cottage was on 8 October 1938, when 49,335 saw Fulham beat Millwall 2–1 in a Second Division game. Viv Woodward and James Evans scored the Cottagers' goals.

ATTENDANCE – LOWEST The lowest-ever attendance at Craven Cottage was on 28 November 1991 when only 1,108 turned up for Gillingham's visit in the Autoglass Trophy. Fulham won 2–0 with goals from Morgan and Cole.

AUTOGLASS TROPHY The Autoglass Trophy replaced the Leyland Daf Cup for the 1991–92 season. Fulham won both of their group matches, beating Maidstone United away 6–1, Gary Brazil netting a hat-trick, and Gillingham at home 2–0. The Gills were Fulham's opponents in the first-round of the competition, a match which the Cottagers also won 2–0, Simon Morgan finding the net in both encounters. In the Southern Area quarter-final, Fulham lost 2–0 at home to Wrexham and went out of the competition. In 1992–93 Fulham met Gillingham for the third time in two seasons in the competition but on this occasion, honours were even with six goals apiece. Jeff Eckhardt, who scored one of Fulham's goals in the game against Gillingham, netted again in the club's other preliminary round game against Leyton Orient, which ended in a 2–2 draw. In the first-round, the Cottagers travelled to Port Vale but lost 4–3 after extra-time to the competition's eventual winners. The following season, Fulham again qualified for the knockout stages of the competition despite losing 1–0 at Reading after their 4–1 defeat of Brighton. The Cottagers then travelled to play Bristol Rovers and, with the game drawn 2–2, won 4–3 on penalties. In the Southern Area quarter-final, a Peter Baah goal gave Fulham a 1–0 win at Reading to avenge the Cottagers' defeat in the preliminary round. Drawn at home to Wycombe Wanderers in the Southern Area semi-final, Fulham were held to a 2–2 draw with Gary Brazil scoring both of the Cottagers' goals before the visitors won 4–2 in the deciding penalty shoot-out.

AUTO WINDSCREEN SHIELD The Auto Windscreen Shield replaced the Autoglass Trophy in the 1994–95 season. For their first match in the newly named competition, Fulham travelled to Leyton Orient where they were well beaten 5–2. Despite this setback, the Cottagers still qualified for the knockout stages of the competition with a 3–2 home win over Colchester United. Drawn away to Leyton Orient again, Fulham put up a much better showing but lost 1–0 to the Brisbane Road club. Despite failing to win a group game in 1995–96 – Wycombe Wanderers (away 1–1) and Walsall (home 2–5) – the Cottagers still managed to qualify for the knockout stages where a Nicky Cusack goal gave them a 1–0 win at Brentford and a place in the Southern Area quarter-final. A Craven Cottage crowd of 3,479 saw Fulham go down 2–1 to Bristol Rovers, a match the Cottagers were unlucky to lose. In 1996–97, Fulham went out of the competition at the first hurdle, losing 3–2 at Brighton and Hove Albion. The game ended all-square at 2–2 but the Seagulls went on to win on the sudden death rule. The following season, Fulham reached the Southern Area quarter-final after victories over Watford 1–0 and Wycombe Wanderers 3–1, but then lost 2–1 to Luton Town for whom Thorpe scored a last-minute winner. Fulham last entered the competition in 1998–99 but went out at the first hurdle, losing 2–1 in extra-time to Torquay.

AWAY MATCHES Fulham's best away win was 8–0 at Halifax Town on 16 September 1969. The club also beat Luton Town 8–3 in an FA Cup first-round match on 11 January 1908. Fulham's worst defeat away from home was the 10–0 League Cup beating meted out by Liverpool on 23 September 1986, whilst the Cottagers' worst defeat in the League was the 9–0 humiliation at the hands of Wolverhampton Wanderers on 16 September 1959. The highest-scoring away match was in 1927–28 when Fulham lost 8–4 at Barnsley.

AWAY SEASONS The club's highest number of away wins came in seasons 1996–97 and 1998–99 when they won 12 of their 23 matches. In 1996–97 the Cottagers finished runners-up to Wigan Athletic to win promotion to Division Two whilst in 1998–99 they won the Second Division Championship. Fulham's fewest away wins (one) occurred in seasons 1923–24, 1927–28, 1964–65 and 1968–69.

B

BACUZZI, JOE The father of David who played for Arsenal, Manchester City and Reading, Joe Bacuzzi began his career playing for Isthmian League club Tufnell Park before turning out in a number of 'A' team games for Arsenal. In 1935, Bacuzzi joined Fulham as an amateur, turning professional the following year. He made his début for the Craven Cottage club in a 4–1 defeat at Chesterfield in January 1937, playing at right-back, whilst his only other appearance that season was at left-back in a 1–0 defeat at Barnsley. Bacuzzi, who scored two goals during his Craven Cottage career, netted the first of these the following season when Luton Town were beaten 4–1. He was ever-present in 1938–39, the last season of league football before the Second World War, and appeared in 104 wartime games for the club. When peacetime football resumed in 1946–47, Bacuzzi was again the club's first choice right-back, taking his total of League and Cup appearances to 299 before a serious knee injury ended his playing career at the end of the 1955–56 season. Appointed the club's trainer, he remained at Craven Cottage in that capacity for a further nine seasons.

BAGGE, HARRY Half-back Harry Bagge joined Tottenham Hotspur as an amateur during the First World War but after being unable to break into the first-team, he joined Fulham. He made his League début in a 1–0 home win over South Shields on the opening day of the 1919–20 season but only appeared in five games that season as the Cottagers finished sixth in Division Two.

It was early the following season when Bagge won a regular place in the Fulham side, going on to miss very few games over the next six seasons. His only goal for the club came in April 1924 as the Cottagers beat Stoke 3–0. During his time at Craven Cottage, Bagge played in 191 League and Cup games before leaving in 1926 to play for Sheffield Wednesday. Unable to break into the Owls' first-team, he left Hillsborough and moved to Spain where he took up a coaching post.

BARRETT, ALBERT After appearing in three English Schools Shield finals for West Ham Boys, Albert Barrett was capped by England Schoolboys before joining Leytonstone in 1921. There he won England Amateur international honours before leaving to have brief spells with West Ham United and Southampton. In the summer of 1925 he joined Fulham as a professional and made his début for the Cottagers in a 4-0 defeat at Oldham Athletic in the fourth game of the 1925–26 season. Barrett went on to miss very few games for Fulham over the next ten seasons, being ever-present in 1930–31 and 1934–35. His performances as an attacking wing-half led to him representing the FA XI in their tour of South Africa in 1929 and his one and only England cap against Northern Ireland the following season. In 1931–32, Barrett helped the Cottagers win the Third Division (South) Championship and the following season was instrumental in Fulham almost winning successive promotion as they finished third in Division Two. He went on to score 21 goals in 418 League and Cup games before hanging up his boots. He then rejoined Leytonstone as coach before later emigrating to South Africa.

BARRETT, LES Speedy winger Les Barrett made his League début for Fulham in a goalless home draw against Blackpool in January 1966 in a season that saw the club struggling to avoid relegation to the Second Division. Despite the Cottagers eventually losing their First Division status in 1967–68, Barrett's performances on the flanks led to him winning England Under-23 international honours against Greece. Disaster struck the following season when the club went straight down into the Third Division and though a number of top flight clubs showed an interest in him, nothing materialised and Barrett remained at Craven Cottage. When the club won promotion in 1970–71, Barrett was not only ever-present but was Fulham's leading scorer with 15 goals. He was still with the club when they reached Wembley in 1975 and won an FA Cup runners-up medal

Les Barrett

after they had been beaten 2–0 by West Ham United. Barrett, whose accurate pin-point crosses created numerous chances for his colleagues, also liked to cut inside and have a go himself and in 491 League and Cup appearances for the Cottagers, he scored 89 goals. He left Craven Cottage in October 1977 to join Millwall for £12,000 but after just eight league appearances for the Lions he headed for the United States before returning to end his career with a spell as player-coach of Woking. After working as a British Telecom engineer, he now runs a garden centre in Earlsfield, south-west London.

BARTON, TONY An England Schoolboy and Youth international, Tony Barton played non-League football for Sutton United before joining Fulham. He made his début in a 4–2 defeat at Lincoln City on the final day of the 1953–54 season. Over the next five seasons, Barton was in and out of the Fulham side and had scored eight goals in 49 games when in December 1959 he was transferred to Nottingham Forest. Unable to settle at the City Ground, he joined Portsmouth and provided many of the crosses which Ron Saunders converted into goals as Pompey won the Third Division title in 1961–62. He stayed with Portsmouth after retiring from the playing side as first-team coach before joining Saunders at Villa Park as his assistant. He was promoted to team manager in February 1982 after Saunders left and guided Villa to a European Cup final victory four months later. He lost his job at Villa Park at the end of the 1983–84 season and joined Northampton Town. Sadly he suffered a heart attack a year later and was forced to leave before recovering and joining Chris Nicholl at Southampton.

BEASLEY, PAT Pat Beasley joined his home-town club Stourbridge before being transferred to Arsenal as a 17-year-old in the summer of 1931. Playing primarily as a winger, he was restricted to reserve-team football due to the consistency of Hulme and Bastin but in 1933–34 he won a regular place and helped the club win the League Championship. In October 1936 he left Highbury to join Huddersfield Town where in three seasons up to the outbreak of World War Two, he appeared in an FA Cup final and won an England cap, scoring the winning goal against Scotland. During the hostilities he 'guested' for Arsenal and won two wartime caps but in December 1945 he left Huddersfield to join Fulham. He made his Cottagers début in a 7–2 defeat at Bury on the opening day of the 1946–47 season. Appointed club captain, he missed very few games in his four seasons with the Cottagers, leading them to the Second Division Championship in 1948–49. He had scored 13 goals in 164 League and Cup games before leaving to become player-manager of Bristol City. He made 66 appearances for the Robins before hanging up his boots to become the Ashton Gate club's manager. The Robins won the Third Division (South) Championship under his managership in 1954–55 but in January 1958 his contract was terminated by mutual agreement. He then joined Birmingham City, initially as joint-manager with Arthur Turner but eight months later became acting manager and then team manager in January 1959. He left St Andrew's in May 1960 and after a spell as Fulham's scout, managed non-League Dover for four years.

BECK, JOHN Edmonton-born midfielder John Beck began his career with Queen's Park Rangers and in three seasons at Loftus Road made 47 first-team appearances before Coventry City paid £40,000 for his services in June 1976. At Highfield Road, Beck gained a reputation as a dead-ball specialist but in October 1978, after making 78 appearances for the Sky Blues, he joined Fulham for £80,000. His first game for the Cottagers was in a 3–0 defeat at Brighton and Hove Albion after which he was a first-team regular for the next three seasons. He had scored 13 goals in 126 League and Cup games when, following the appointment of Malcolm Macdonald as manager, he was dropped. Beck moved to Bournemouth where he won an Associate Members' Cup winners' medal before leaving to end his playing career with Cambridge United. When United manager Chris Turner resigned in 1990, Beck took over as caretaker manager and became the first caretaker manager to win a divisional manager of the month award twice in succession. He took full control as Cambridge reached the quarter-final of the FA Cup and won promotion to the Third Division via the play-offs. The following year the Abbey Stadium club ended the season as the Third Division Champions and in 1991–92 they just missed out on a place in the top-flight, losing in the play-offs. In December 1992 he became manager of Preston North End, leading the club to the Third Division play-offs in 1993–94. He later managed Lincoln City but lost his job in 1998.

BEECHAM, ERNEST Goalkeeper Ernest Beecham began his career with non-League Hertford Town in the Spartan League before joining Fulham as an amateur in October 1923 and signing professional forms six months later. He played his first match for the Cottagers in a 2–0 defeat at Blackpool in December 1925, going on to appear in 122 consecutive League games from his début. Also in his first season he produced a series of outstanding saves as Second Division Fulham reached the FA Cup sixth round before losing 2–1 to Manchester United. Beecham, who was ever-present in seasons 1926–27 and 1927–28, toured Holland with an

John Beck

England XI though he was unfortunate not to win full honours for his country. During the goalless home draw against Exeter City in November 1928, Beecham damaged his spine diving at the feet of an onrushing Grecian forward. It was an injury that not only forced him to miss the rest of that campaign but one that troubled him throughout the rest of his career. Beecham went on to make 185 League and Cup appearances for Fulham before being transferred to Queen's Park Rangers in the summer of 1932. He was their first-choice keeper for three seasons and had appeared in 95 games before breaking his arm in the match against Charlton Athletic. He had decided to retire when Brighton and Hove Albion persuaded him to join them. He later had a spell with Swindon Town before managing Ware of the Spartan League.

BENTLEY, ROY Roy Bentley began his Football League career as an inside-forward with Newcastle United after playing for both Bristol clubs during the Second World War. But when he joined Chelsea in January 1948, he was tried at centre-forward and with great success. He captained the Stamford Bridge club to the League Championship in 1954–55 and gained many honours whilst with the Pensioners. He appeared in the 1950 World Cup in Brazil and in 12 games for England scored nine goals including a hat-trick in a 3–1 win over Wales. He had scored 150 goals in 366 League and Cup games for Chelsea when he left to join Fulham in September 1956 for a fee of £8,600. Bentley scored on his début for the Cottagers in a 3–1 home win over Rotherham United and ended the season with 14 goals in 32 games including a hat-trick in a 6–3 defeat of Port Vale. Midway through the 1957–58 season, Bentley was converted into an outstanding half-back and the following campaign was instrumental in Fulham winning promotion to the First Division. He had scored 25 goals in 160 games for the Cottagers when he moved to Queen's Park Rangers, where he ended his playing career. Appointed manager of Reading, he reorganised the then Elm Park club and experimented with new methods of play. The Berkshire club finished consecutive seasons in fourth and fifth position in Division Three in 1967 and 1968 but after a poor season in 1968–69, he left the club. Bentley took over at Swansea in August 1969 and at the end of his first season at Vetch Field, had led the club to promotion to the Third Division. After two seasons of mid-table placings the Swans made a poor start to the 1972–73 campaign and Bentley was sacked. After managing non-League Thatcham Town, Bentley later held the post of secretary at both Reading and Aldershot.

BEST, GEORGE Soccer superstar George Best began his career with Manchester United, making his League début against West Bromwich Albion in September 1963. After only 15 games, Northern Ireland gave him his first cap in the match against Wales at Swansea. Best initially played wide on the left but soon began to play in a free attacking role, scoring some of the most stunning goals ever seen at Old Trafford. He won a League Championship medal in 1965 and again in 1967, though the peak of Best's career came in 1968 when United won the European Cup at Wembley, beating Benfica 4–1 after extra-time. It was a euphoric night for United and for Best, the pinnacle of achievement in a season that saw him gain the titles of English and European Footballer of the Year. Unable to cope with the pressures of stardom, he walked out on United several times and played his last game for them on New Year's Day 1974 at Queen's Park Rangers. Four days later he failed to turn up for training yet again and his days at Old Trafford were over. In November 1975 he joined Stockport County on loan before heading for the United States, playing for Los Angeles Aztecs. In September 1976 he joined Fulham and scored the only goal of the game on his début as Bristol Rovers were beaten 1–0. He went on to score ten goals in 47 games before arguments over money saw him return to the States to play for San Diego Sockers, Fort Lauderdale Strikers and San Jose Earthquakes in the NASL. In

George Best

1980–81 he played Scottish League football for Hibernian and later Motherwell. He also turned out for Glentoran, Bournemouth and several non-League clubs. George Best was a footballing genius and has gone down in history as one of world football's all-time greats.

BEST STARTS The Cottagers were unbeaten for the first 12 games of the 1958–59 Second Division promotion-winning season when they won nine and drew three of their matches. Their first defeat came at home to Liverpool on 18 October 1958 when they went down 1–0.

BIRCH, JOE Born in Hednesford, defender Joe Birch began his Football League career with Birmingham in 1927 but after just one appearance for the St Andrew's club, he left to play for Bournemouth. Injuries restricted his appearances in his first season at Dean Court but he returned in 1930–31 to produce a series of performances that alerted the attention of a number of clubs. It was Fulham manager James McIntyre who signed Birch in the summer of 1931, the strong-tackling defender making his début in a 1–1 home draw against Southend United in October 1931. Birch, who was equally at home in either full-back position went on to play in 32 games that season as the Cottagers won the Third Division (South) Championship. Birch was a regular in the Fulham side for the next six seasons, appearing in 197 League and Cup games before leaving Craven Cottage in July 1938 to see out his career with Colchester United.

BLACK, IAN Goalkeeper Ian Black had his first taste of professional football with his home-town club Aberdeen and then Chelsea during the later stages of the Second World War. When he was demobbed he asked Aberdeen to release him to Southampton where he had found employment as a mechanic. The Scottish club, appreciating Black's talents, were reluctant to let him go and Bill Dodgin was lucky to be able to recruit such an excellent keeper. Within a few months of arriving at The Dell, Black had won a Scottish cap against England. In August 1950, after appearing in 97 games for the Saints, Black followed Dodgin to Fulham and made his début for the Cottagers in a 1–0 defeat at Manchester United on the opening day of the 1950–51 season. Black was ever-present during that campaign and in eight seasons at Craven Cottage missed very few games. In the second game of the 1952–53 season, Black became the only goalkeeper ever to score for Fulham in a League game. Replacing an injured player in the match at Leicester City, he was moved to centre-forward and scored the Cottagers' only goal in a 6–1 defeat. Black had played in 277 League and Cup games for Fulham when, after losing his place to Tony Macedo, he left to play Southern League football for Bath City.

BLAKE, MARK An England Youth international, defender Mark Blake began his League career with Southampton, coming into the Saints' side at the tail end of the 1985–86 season due to a spate of injuries that had deprived Southampton of their entire defence. He went on to make 26 first-team appearances but, following a spell on loan to Colchester United, he joined Shrewsbury Town for £100,000 in March 1990. Blake spent four seasons with the Gay Meadow club, making 175 appearances before a free transfer took him to Fulham in September 1994. He made his début as a substitute in a 5–1 defeat at Walsall before making the starting line-up the following week against Hereford United (home 1–1). Over the next four seasons he proved himself to be one of the club's most consistent players. Dangerous at set pieces and an excellent reader of the game, he was instrumental in the club winning promotion to the Second Division in 1996–97. He had scored 19 goals in 167 games for the Cottagers when he left to play for French side Cannes in the summer of 1998.

BRACEWELL, PAUL A superb passer of the ball, Paul Bracewell played well for Stoke for three full seasons before following manager Alan Durban to Sunderland for £250,000 in the summer of 1983. Things didn't work out for him at Roker Park and after just one season he moved to Everton. Bracewell holds the rare distinction of making his Everton début at Wembley, where he played in the Charity Shield showpiece against Liverpool in August 1984. Forming a good understanding with Peter Reid in the Everton midfield, he won his first full England cap when he replaced Bryan Robson against West Germany on the summer tour to Mexico. On New Year's Day 1986, Bracewell suffered a serious injury to his right ankle at Newcastle United and was out of action for more than twenty months. During this time he had five operations and, after returning to the first-team towards the end of the 1987–88 season, had to undergo still more surgery on the damaged ankle. He appeared in 135 first-team games, winning League Championship and European Cup Winners' Cup medals and in 1989 rejoined Sunderland for a transfer fee of £250,000. He played for the Wearsiders in the 1992 FA Cup final

Paul Bracewell

– the fourth time he had picked up a runners-up medal – before joining Newcastle United. He made a telling contribution to the Magpies' promotion to the Premier League before returning to Sunderland for his third spell and helping the club return to the top-flight as First Division champions. In October 1997, the veteran midfielder joined Fulham for £75,000 and made his début in a 1–0 home win over Blackpool. He went on to play in the remaining 36 games of the season as Fulham reached the Second Division play-offs, only to lose over two legs to Grimsby

Town. Appointed the club's player-coach, he had helped the Cottagers reach first place in Division Two in 1998–99 when injury forced him to miss a couple of months at the end of the season. Bracewell appeared in 76 games for the Cottagers, scoring his only goal for them in a 2–0 win over Wycombe Wanderers in September 1998. When Kevin Keegan left to take the England job full-time, Bracewell was appointed the club's manager but despite taking them to the fringe of the First Division play-off places, he was sacked in March 2000.

BRADSHAW, HARRY Harry Bradshaw was Fulham's first full-time manager and one of the most successful. He first made his name as a player with Burnley, later becoming that club's secretary as they won the Second Division Championship in 1897–98. In June 1899, Bradshaw was appointed manager of Woolwich Arsenal and in a short space of time he brought about a remarkable transformation in the Gunners' fortunes. Not only did they win promotion to the First Division but their slide towards bankruptcy was also halted. Therefore it came as a great surprise when he left to manage Fulham in the summer of 1904. He led the Cottagers to the Southern League Championship in seasons 1905–06 and 1906–07, into the Football League and to an FA Cup semi-final. After five years with the club during which time he had also helped in the redevelopment of Craven Cottage, Bradshaw decided not to extend his contract when it expired in 1909 and chose to become the secretary of the Southern League instead.

BRADSHAW, JOE As a player, winger Joe Bradshaw made little impact at both Fulham and Chelsea but helped Southend United regain their place in the First Division of the Southern League. Bradshaw was player-manager at Roots Hall until the outbreak of the First World War but then left to join the army. On his demob he was appointed manager of Swansea and almost immediately piloted the Swans into the Football League. In 1924–25 he guided the Welsh club to the Third Division (South) Championship and the following season the club won through to the semi-finals of the FA Cup where they lost to Bolton Wanderers. He left the Vetch Field in May 1926 to manage Fulham but he had a difficult time at Craven Cottage and in 1927–28 the club were relegated for the first time in their history. Though the Cottagers scored 101 goals in 1928-29 and finished fifth in the Third Division (South) it wasn't enough to save his job and he was sacked. He then took charge at Bristol City but in 1931–32, after only three victories in 32 matches, he was dismissed with the Ashton Gate club in a desperate financial position.

BRANFOOT, IAN After playing his early football with his hometown team Gateshead, Ian Branfoot had a few games for Sheffield Wednesday before joining Doncaster Rovers in 1969. He went on to make 156 appearances for the Belle Vue club before moving to Lincoln City in the summer of 1973. At Sincil Bank he was ever-present as the Imps won the Fourth Division Championship in 1975–76 but after making 166 appearances for them he retired to become their coach. After a brief spell as coach to Southampton, Branfoot became manager of Reading, helping them to win promotion to Division Three in 1983–84 and win the Third Division Championship two seasons later. However, after just one season in Division Two, the Royals were relegated and in a struggle to avoid a second successive relegation, Branfoot was sacked. He then acted as assistant manager to Steve Coppell at Crystal Palace before being appointed manager of Southampton in June 1991. He took the Saints to the Zenith Data Systems Cup final where they lost to Nottingham Forest but their form in the League was disappointing and after three seasons of struggling to avoid relegation, he parted company with the south-coast club. Branfoot was appointed manager of Fulham in June 1994, the Cottagers finishing eighth in Division Three at the end of his first season in charge. With the club struggling in the lower reaches of the Third Division the following season, player-coach Micky Adams was given full responsibility for team affairs with Ian Branfoot becoming general manager.

BRENNAN, BOBBY Belfast-born inside-forward Bobby Brennan began his footballing career with Distillery where he won an Irish Cup runners-up medal and represented the Irish League. In October 1947 he joined Luton Town for £3,000 and had scored 22 goals in 67 League appearances when he left Kenilworth Road to sign for Birmingham City for £20,000 in the summer of 1949. However, after just one season at St Andrew's, he left the Blues to join Fulham for £19,500. He made his début for the Cottagers in a 1–0 defeat at Manchester United on the opening day of the 1950–51 season and over the next three campaigns, scored 16 goals in 80 games before losing his place to Johnny Haynes. Brennan, who was capped five times by Northern Ireland, signed for Norwich City and scored the only goal of the game against Southend United on his Canaries' début. After ending the season as the club's joint top scorer he went on to become the leading scorer in 1954–55 with 11 goals in 38 games. He was released under Tom Parker's management and went to play for Yarmouth Town but was re-signed after the new Norwich board took over in February 1957. He went on to score 52 goals in 250 League and Cup games for the Carrow Road club after which he took up a coaching post with King's Lynn.

BRICE, GORDON Gordon Brice began his Football League career with Luton Town but after scoring 13 goals in 46 games for the Hatters, he left to join Wolverhampton Wanderers in the summer of 1947 for a fee of £10,000. Groomed as Stan Cullis's successor, Brice failed to settle at Molineux and was happy to join Reading ten months later. He spent just over four seasons at Elm Park appearing in 198 league games before Fulham manager Bill Dodgin senior brought him to Craven Cottage. He made his début for the Cottagers in a 3–1 home win over Swansea Town in April 1953 whilst the following season, he was one of four ever-presents in the Fulham side. In February 1955, Brice scored his only goal for the club in a 2–1 home defeat by Liverpool. He had appeared in 93 League and Cup games for Fulham when in the summer of 1956 he left Craven Cottage to end his career playing Scottish League football for Ayr United.

BROTHERS There have been three instances of brothers playing for Fulham. Three of the five Farnfield brothers, G.S., H.V. and P.H. 'guested' for the Cottagers in the final Southern League game of the 1903–04 season, a 1–1 home draw against West Ham United. They all played for Cambridge University and Clapton whilst PH Farnfield won England Amateur honours against France in 1907 and represented the Amateurs against the Professionals at Craven Cottage. HV Farnfield later became a priest. Billy Goldie joined Fulham from Liverpool in January 1904, having won a League Championship medal whilst with the Reds. During his five seasons at Craven Cottage he rarely missed a match, winning two Southern League Championship medals in the process. He had appeared in 179 games when in 1908 he left to join Leicester Fosse. His brother 'Jock', who was a similar type of player, made 33 appearances before leaving to play for Glossop and later Bury. Whilst with the Shakers he was banned for life from football for his part in a fixed game between Bury and Coventry City. Jimmy Conway began his career with Irish League club Bohemians before moving to Fulham in the summer of 1966. A Republic of Ireland international with 19 caps, he helped the club win promotion in 1970–71 and was a member of the Fulham side that reached the FA Cup final in 1975. More of a provider of goals, he still found the net 76 times in his 360 appearances for the club. His brother John followed him to Craven Cottage and though he was unlucky with injuries, 19 of his 45 appearances for the club were in the same side as his brother Jimmy.

BROWN, ARTHUR Arthur Brown, who at 18 was England's youngest international until Duncan Edwards made his début in 1955, began his career with his home-town team, Gainsborough Trinity. Sheffield United soon saw his potential and took him to Bramall Lane where in six seasons for the Yorkshire club, he scored 96 goals in 174 games. In June 1908, Brown moved to Sunderland for what was at the time a world record fee of £1,600. After netting 20 goals in 42 games in his first season at Roker Park, he lost his place midway through the 1909–10 season. Fulham manager Phil Kelso brought him to Craven Cottage in October 1910 and he made his début in a 1–1 draw at Stockport County. Injuries hampered his progress in his two seasons with the Cottagers and he was never quite able to reproduce the form of his Sheffield United days. He had scored 12 goals in 46 games when he left to end his career with Middlesbrough.

BROWN, HARRY Harry Brown started his career in 1902 with Northampton Town before signing for West Bromwich Albion prior to the 1904–05 season. His stay at the Hawthorns was brief and in April 1905 he signed for Southampton. He spent a fine season at The Dell but was anxious to move back into the Football League. Brown signed for Newcastle United in 1906 and in his first season at St James Park, helped the Magpies win the League Championship. In October 1907 he was on the move again, this time to Bradford Park Avenue, but five months later he left the Yorkshire club to join Fulham. His first game for the Cottagers saw him score twice in a 5–1 home win over Leicester Fosse. He ended the season with five goals in seven games including a hat-trick in a 5–1 defeat of Stoke. Brown continued to be an important member of the Fulham side until September 1910 when, after scoring 21 goals in 55 games, he rejoined Southampton. After two more seasons at The Dell, he retired due to poor eyesight and ran a pub in the town, purchased from ex-Saint Tom Nicol. Sadly, Brown later went blind and died in Nuneaton in 1934 at the age of 50.

BROWN, ROGER Tamworth-born defender Roger Brown joined

his local club Walsall as an apprentice but after being unable to break into the Saddlers' first-team, left to play as a semi-professional for AP Leamington. After a series of outstanding performances, his Football League career was resurrected when Bournemouth signed him in February 1978. He had made 63 League appearances for the Cherries when First Division Norwich City spotted his potential and signed him in the summer of 1979 for £85,000. Eight months later, Brown, who couldn't settle at Carrow Road, joined Fulham for a fee of £100,000, making his début in a 2–1 home defeat by Chelsea. Over the next four seasons, Brown became a great favourite with the Craven Cottage faithful and in 1981–82 when the club won promotion to the Second Division, he scored 12 goals from his position at centre-half. One of these came in the win over Lincoln City on the final day of the season to ensure promotion. After scoring 19 goals in 161 games, a disagreement with manager Malcolm Macdonald led to him rejoining Bournemouth where he won an Associate Members Cup winners' medal and took his tally of goals in his two spells to eight in 147 league appearances.

BROWN, STAN Utility player Stan Brown made his Fulham début in the 6-1 home defeat by Sheffield Wednesday on 21 January 1961, a match in which England international Alan Mullery scored an own-goal after just half a minute's play! That was his only game over the next two seasons but in 1962–63 he established himself in the Fulham side and was a first-team regular for the next ten seasons. An ever-present in the club's relegation season of 1967–68, he was instrumental in the club winning promotion to the Second Division three seasons later. He had played in 397 League and Cup games, scoring 19 goals for Fulham when he left Craven Cottage in October 1972 to join Brighton and Hove Albion on loan. The Seagulls were unwilling to take Brown on a permanent basis and two months later he signed for Colchester United. After 23 League appearances for the Layer Road club, then he moved to Southern League Wimbledon. In his only season with the Plough Lane club, the Dons for the only time in their history lost more games than they won! He ended his involvement with the game as player-manager with Haywards Heath in the Sussex League.

BUCKINGHAM, VIC In sixteen years as a player with Tottenham Hotspur, Vic Buckingham never played in the First Division, a record which may show why this tall, stylish player later sought and achieved success as a coach and manager. After making his début against Bury in November 1935, he became established at half-back but like so many of his generation, the best years of his career were lost to the war. Serving in the RAF, he 'guested' for other clubs, even playing for Portsmouth against Spurs and appeared for England in two wartime internationals. He continued to play for Spurs until 1949 when, after 234 first-team outings, he took to coaching the juniors. In June 1951 his talents were recognised by Bradford Park Avenue and he became their manager. In February 1953 he took over at West Bromwich Albion and in his first year they won the FA Cup and finished runners-up in Division One. On leaving the Hawthorns, he coached Ajax of Amsterdam before returning to England to manage Sheffield Wednesday. In January 1965 he took charge at Craven Cottage but after three years of struggling to avoid relegation to the Second Division, he left. Buckingham, who had tried to make too many changes too soon, later managed Ethnikos of Greece and Spanish clubs, Barcelona and Sevilla.

BULLIVANT, TERRY Terry Bullivant made his Fulham début as a substitute for John Dowie in a 3–1 defeat at Bristol City in the last game of the 1974–75 season. The following campaign he appeared in just three League games but midway through the 1976–77 season, the strong-tackling midfielder won a regular place in the Cottagers' side. A great favourite with the Fulham faithful, Bullivant had appeared in 115 League and Cup games when in November 1979 he was allowed to join Aston Villa for a fee of £220,000. His time at Villa Park was not a happy one for, in two and a half seasons, he made just 14 appearances! In July 1982, Bullivant joined Charlton Athletic but after 30 appearances in his only season with the club, he moved to Brentford. Despite a loan spell with Reading, Bullivant made 37 appearances for the Bees and played in their 1985 Freight Rover Trophy side that lost to Wigan Athletic. In the summer of 1986, Bullivant returned to Craven Cottage as part-time youth team coach before a year later being appointed first-team coach. He later had a brief spell as caretaker manager of Barnet where he still coaches.

BUSBY, VIV Following an unsuccessful trial with Fulham, Viv Busby joined his local club, Wycombe Wanderers where his performances attracted the attention of Luton Town. Early on in his Kenilworth Road career, Busby was loaned out to First Division Newcastle United but his spell at St James Park coincided with the club's most embarrassing post-war defeat at the hands of non-League Hereford United. He returned to play for

Luton and had scored 16 goals in 77 games when Fulham signed Busby and Alan Slough for a combined fee of £25,000 in the summer of 1973. He made his Cottagers début in a 2–0 home win over Millwall on the opening day of the 1973–74 season, going on to top score with 12 goals, a total which included a hat-trick in a 4–1 defeat of Sheffield Wednesday. He headed the club's scoring charts again the following season and scored some important goals in the club's run to the FA Cup final. In September 1976, after scoring 37 goals in 143 games, Busby moved to Norwich City for a fee of £50,000. On leaving Carrow Road, Busby played for a number of other clubs, namely Stoke City, Sheffield United (on loan), Tulsa Roughnecks, Blackburn Rovers and York City. On hanging up his boots, he became assistant manager at Bootham Crescent, a position he later held at Sunderland. After acting as a scout for Manchester City, Busby became manager of Hartlepool United before returning to work as a scout for several clubs including Southampton and West Bromwich Albion.

C

CALLAGHAN, FRED Fulham-born defender Fred Callaghan joined the Cottagers ground-staff before signing professional forms in the summer of 1962. After working his way through the ranks, he made his first-team début as a wing-half in a 2–2 draw at Aston Villa in March 1964. Over the next three seasons, he appeared in only 32 first-team games, but following his conversion to left-back, he was a first-team regular for the next seven seasons. He helped the club win promotion to the Second Division in 1970–71 and then in the final game of the following season scored probably his most important goal for the Cottagers when he equalised in the dying minutes at The Valley – a goal which sent Charlton into the Third Division instead of Fulham! Fred Callaghan had scored 12 goals in 336 League and Cup games when a slipped disc forced him to leave first-class football. After a number of seasons managing non-League clubs Enfield and Woking and driving a taxi, he entered League management with Brentford but after three seasons of mid-table mediocrity, he was sacked. He rejoined Woking and led them to promotion to the Vauxhall Conference Premier Division. Now manager of Carshalton, he still drives a London taxi.

CAMPBELL, BOBBY Bobby Campbell began his career with Liverpool where, after winning England Youth international honours, he made just 14 appearances before joining Portsmouth. He had appeared in 68 games for the Fratton Park club but in the summer of 1966 he moved to Aldershot where sadly injury later ended his playing career. He then turned to coaching, first with Portsmouth and then with Queen's Park Rangers where, working alongside Gordon Jago, he helped the Loftus Road club win promotion to the First Division. In 1974 he joined Arsenal in a similar capacity to work with Bertie Mee and though there were those who thought he might replace Mee when the Arsenal boss left two years later, Campbell moved to Craven Cottage, initially as coach to manager Alec Stock. When Stock was forced to leave the club following boardroom pressure, Campbell replaced him. Unfortunately the club's results deteriorated under Campbell's managership and though he made almost £1 million profit in transfer fees, the team never really rose above mid-table. Following a poor start to the 1980–81 season, Campbell was sacked. He became Portsmouth's manager in March 1982 and in his first full season in charge took the club to the Third Division Championship. His reward was a three-year contract to go with his award of Third Division Manager of the Season. Surprisingly, after a season of consolidation, Campbell was sacked with just one game of the 1983–84 season to play. After brief spells at Arsenal and Queen's Park Rangers, he became Chelsea's manager after joining the club as coach to John Hollins. He led the Stamford Bridge club to the Second Division Championship and briefly to the top of the First Division midway through the following season but after the club's defeat by Sheffield Wednesday in the League Cup semi-finals of 1990–91, he was sacked. He is now coaching in Saudi Arabia.

CAMPBELL, JOHNNY Northern Ireland international Johnny Campbell began his professional career with Derry Celtic before moving to Belfast Celtic in 1945. In a little over three seasons with the club, Campbell scored over 100 goals including a three-minute hat-trick against Shelbourne, a performance that helped him to become Irish Footballer of the Year in 1946. In 1946–47 he won an Irish Cup winners' medal as Belfast Celtic defeated Glentoran 1–0. In March 1949, after the Irish club had folded, Campbell, along with Hugh Kelly and Robin Lawler joined the Cottagers. He made his début in a goalless draw at Blackpool seven months after arriving at Craven Cottage. Campbell, who won two full caps for Northern Ireland whilst with Fulham, appeared in all the forward positions for the Cottagers and had scored six goals in 68 League and Cup games when a serious illness forced him to retire in 1953.

CAPACITY The total capacity of Craven Cottage in season 1999–2000 was 19,250.

CAPS (ENGLAND) The first Fulham player to be capped by England was Frank Osborne when he played against Northern Ireland in October 1922. The most capped player is Johnny Haynes with 56 caps.

CAPS (NORTHERN IRELAND) The first Fulham player to be capped by Northern Ireland was Joe Connor when he played against England in March 1904. The most capped players are George Best and Ted Hinton with five caps.

CAPS (REPUBLIC OF IRELAND) The first Fulham player to be capped by the Republic of Ireland was Robin Lawler when he played against Austria in March 1953. The most capped player is goalkeeper Gerry Peyton with 22 caps.

CAPS (SCOTLAND) The first Fulham player to be capped by Scotland was Jimmy Sharp when he played against Wales in March 1909. The most capped player is Graham Leggatt with 11 caps.

CAPS (WALES) The first Fulham player to be capped by Wales was Billy Richards when he played against Northern Ireland in December 1932. The most capped players are Gordon Davies and Jeff Hopkins with 14 caps.

CAPTAINS Among the many players who have captained the club are Jack Fryer, the goalkeeper who played in three losing FA Cup finals for Derby County. He captained the Cottagers to two Southern League Championships in 1905–06 and 1906–07. When Fulham won their first divisional championship, the Third Division (South) in 1931–32, they were captained by Len Oliver, one of the club's stalwarts during the inter-war period. Whilst at Craven Cottage, he became one of the few players to be capped for England whilst playing in the Third Division. Pat Beasley captained the Cottagers to the Second Division Championship in 1948–49 after having won a League Championship medal with Arsenal before the Second World War. An England international he later joined Bristol City as player-manager. Alan Mullery, who had two spells with Fulham, captained the club in their only ever appearance in an FA Cup final – most appropriate as he had been the driving force behind the club's run to the Twin Towers in that

1974–75 season. Simon Morgan was the club's inspirational skipper when they won promotion to the Second Division in 1996–97 as runners-up to Wigan Athletic. When the club won the Second Division Championship with a record 101 points in 1998–99, they were captained by Welsh international Chris Coleman, whose performances won him selection for the award-winning PFA side.

CELEBRITIES The Cottagers have a reputation for unpredictability and eccentricity, partly through their well-publicised association with comedian Tommy Trinder who was the club's chairman for a good number of years. Other celebrities to have joined the board include singer Alan Price, whilst Honor Blackman is a great fan of the Cottagers. One of the recent celebrities to appear at Craven Cottage was Michael Jackson.

CENTURIES There are six instances of individual players who scored 100 or more league goals for Fulham. Gordon Davies is the leading goalscorer with 159 strikes in his Craven Cottage career. Other centurions are Bedford Jezzard (154), Johnny Haynes (146), Jim Hammond (141), Graham Leggatt (127) and Arthur Stevens (110). Les Barrett holds the club record for the most consecutive League appearances – 148. Other players to have made over 100 consecutive appearances during their careers are Ernest Beecham (122), Arthur Reynolds (120), Barry Lloyd (119), Bedford Jezzard (115), Syd Gibbons (114), Jim Langley (114), Peter Mellor (108), John Dempsey (107) and Gerry Peyton (105).

CHAMBERLAIN, 'TOSH' A former England Schoolboy international who once scored a hat-trick in the space of four minutes against the Republic of Ireland, 'Tosh' Chamberlain joined Fulham's ground-staff in 1948, winning England Youth honours shortly afterwards. Following two years National Service, Chamberlain made his league début for the Cottagers against Lincoln City on 20 November 1954. He made a sensational start, scoring inside the first minute with his first kick as Fulham went on to win 3–2. Midway through the following season, Chamberlain established himself in the club's first-team. In one of the most exciting FA Cup games seen at Craven Cottage, he netted a memorable hat-trick against Newcastle United but the Magpies won 5–4. Later in that 1955–56 campaign, he scored his first League hat-trick as Fulham beat Doncaster Rovers 4–0. The following season was Chamberlain's best in terms of goals. He scored a total of 15 in 39 games including another hat-trick in a 7–2 rout of Blackburn Rovers on Boxing Day 1956. Forming an outstanding left-wing partnership with Johnny Haynes, Chamberlain went on to score 64 goals in 204 games for the Cottagers before deciding to retire.

CHAMPIONSHIPS Fulham have won a divisional championship on three occasions. First in 1931–32 when the club finished two points ahead of runners-up Reading to win the Third Division (South) Championship. The club's leading scorer was Frank 'Bonzo' Newton with a record 43 goals including three hat-tricks. The Cottagers beat Torquay United 10–2, a match in which Jim Hammond scored four of the goals, and Thames 8–0 with Hammond netting a hat-trick. In 1948–49, Fulham pipped West Bromwich Albion and Southampton for the Second Division title. The club had played just four matches when manager Jack Peart tragically died following a short illness. His replacement Frank Osborne brought in Bedford Jezzard and exchanged Ernie Shepherd for West Bromwich Albion's Arthur Rowley, with the latter scoring 19 goals in 22 appearances. Fulham took 21 points out of a possible 26 to take the title, a point ahead of the Baggies. Finally, in 1998–99 the club won the Second Division Championship with a record 101 points, 14 ahead of runners-up Walsall. During the course of the season, Fulham established two club records – the longest sequence of unbeaten League matches (15) and the longest sequence of League wins (8). Shortly afterwards, manager Kevin Keegan left Craven Cottage to become England team manager.

CHAPLIN, ALEC Alec Chaplin played his early football with Dundee Hibernian before moving to London early in the First World War to work in Napiers munitions factory. He was recommended to Tottenham Hotspur by his elder brother and former Spurs full-back John Chaplin and he played in four of the first five matches of the London Football Combination. After that he was not seen in Spurs' colours again and instead turned out for the factory side. It was whilst playing for them in 1919, that Chaplin was spotted by Fulham and after agreeing terms went straight into the first-team when normal football resumed, succeeding his brother-in-law, Jimmy Sharp. Appointed club captain, Chaplin was the club's first-choice left-back for seven seasons, appearing in 276 League and Cup games. His only goal for the Cottagers came in March 1924 when Fulham lost 2–1 at Leicester City. When Joe Bradshaw was appointed Fulham's manager, Chaplin moved to become player-coach at the Northfleet Nursery, helping them win the Kent Senior Cup twice in the space of three years. Later in life he served for 15 years as a member of Fulham Council.

CHARLTON, TED Ted Charlton joined Fulham in the summer of 1906 and made his début in a 1–1 draw at Plymouth Argyle. At the end of that season he had made 20 appearances and won a Southern League Championship medal. During 1907–08, the club's first season in the Football League, Charlton had a major disagreement with the management and almost left to play for Glossop. However, despite the transfer being blocked, he failed to win a place in the Cottagers' League side and spent most of the season in the reserves. Having made his League début in a 6–1 defeat of Glossop, Charlton won a regular place in 1908–09, a season in which he played in an international trial match. The following season he won a London Challenge Cup winners' medal and was the club's first-choice left-back up until the outbreak of the First World War. When League football resumed in 1919–20, Charlton was still a member of the Fulham side but after having appeared in 229 League games he was injured in the match against Blackpool and forced to retire.

CLARK, LEE An England player at Schools, Youth and Under-21 level, Lee Clark began his League career with Newcastle United. He was given his chance in the Magpies' first-team by Ossie Ardiles in 1990–91 and established himself as a first-team regular the following season. Following the club's promotion to the Premier League in 1992–93, when he was ever-present, he found himself frustrated at not getting a regular place in Kevin Keegan's line-up. He did return to take his tally of goals to 26 in 228 games before becoming Sunderland's record signing when they paid £2.75 million for his services in the summer of 1997. He capped a superb first year with the Wearsiders as an ever-present by being named in the Division One select team. Sadly, on the opening day of the 1998–99 season, he broke his leg in the match against Queen's Park Rangers but returned four months later to help the Wearsiders win the First Division Championship. Selected for the PFA First Division side for a second year running, Clark, who had scored 16 goals in 82 games for Sunderland, was surprisingly sold to Fulham for £3 million in July 1999.

CLARKE, ALLAN An instinctive goalscorer, Allan Clarke came from a footballing family – brothers Wayne, Frank, Derek and Kelvin all played League football – but he was the pick of the crop. He represented Birmingham Schools and South East Staffordshire Boys before joining Walsall as an apprentice in 1961, turning professional in August 1963. He began knocking in goals and in March 1966, he joined First Division Fulham for £35,000. He made his début as a substitute for Johnny Haynes in a 3–1 home defeat by Leeds United before making his first full appearance in the return match at Elland Road four days later as the Cottagers gained revenge with a 1–0 win. In 1966–67, Clarke was Fulham's leading scorer with 29 League and Cup goals, a total which included a hat-trick in a 5–1 home win over Newcastle United. He topped the charts again the following season, scoring four times in a 6–2 League Cup defeat of Workington. Following Fulham's relegation in 1968, Clarke, who had scored 57 goals in 100 games, demanded a move and Leicester City paid a club record £150,000 for his services. He soon ingratiated himself to the Filbert Street faithful with a hat-trick in a 3–0 win over Manchester City and the FA Cup semi-final winner against West Bromwich Albion. Voted the Man of the Match in Leicester's 1969 FA Cup final defeat by Manchester City, he had scored 16 goals in 46 games when Leeds United boss Don Revie paid £165,000 to take him to Elland Road. Nicknamed 'Sniffer' in recognition of his clinical penalty-area poaching skills, he played in three FA Cup finals for the Yorkshire club – scoring the winning goal in 1972 – won a League Championship medal in 1974 and was also scorer in their Inter Cities Fairs Cup victory of 1971. Clarke, who won 19 full caps for England, had scored 151 goals in 366 games for Leeds when in June 1978 he left to become player-manager of Barnsley. After helping the Oakwell club out of the Fourth Division in his first year of management, he returned to Leeds as boss, subsequently also managing Scunthorpe United, Barnsley again and Lincoln City.

CLARKE, BRUCE Though he was born in Johannesburg, South Africa, Bruce Clarke spent most of his childhood in Scotland. He played his early football for the Hillside Junior Club before later playing for Montrose and Third Lanark. It was his performances for the latter club that impressed a Fulham scout and in the summer of 1934 he joined the Cottagers for a fee of £550. A versatile player, he made his début at outside-right in a 3–0 home win over Plymouth Argyle on the opening day of the 1934–35 season. That campaign saw him miss just two games and score his only goal for the club in a 4–1 home win over Blackpool. Clarke, who also appeared at right-half and inside-forward, found his first-team appearances restricted following the signing of James Evans from Arsenal in 1937, but stayed at Craven Cottage until the outbreak of the Second World War. He had appeared in 114 first-team games when he left the club to return to his work as a joiner.

CLEAN SHEETS This is the colloquial expression used to describe a goalkeeper's performance when he does not concede a goal. When the Cottagers won the Second Division Championship in 1998–99, Maik Taylor had 23 clean sheets in 46 League appearances.

COCK, DONALD Although Donald Cock was a prolific goalscorer in his own right, he had to live in the shadow of his brother, Jack, a goalscoring phenomenon with Huddersfield Town, Chelsea, Everton and England. Cock was playing for Brentford during the First World War before joining Fulham in the summer of 1919. He scored both the Cottagers' goals on his début in a 3–2 defeat at Leicester City, going on to score 11 goals in his first five games including a hat-trick in the 5–0 win over Leicester City in the return match. He ended the season with 25 goals in 33 games and was the club's leading scorer. In his three seasons at Craven Cottage, Cock scored 44 goals in 93 games before being transferred to Notts County. He was the club's leading scorer in 1922–23 and 1923–24 as well as helping County to the Second Division Championship in 1922–23. In March 1925, Arsenal paid a club record fee of £4,000 for his services but in only his second game against his former club, Notts County, he was tackled heavily and broke a leg. Though he recovered fully, he played just one more game before being transferred to Clapton Orient where he topped the club's scoring charts in his two seasons at Homerton. Cock was one of only a few players to have been three different clubs' leading League goalscorer in two or more seasons.

COHEN, GEORGE England international full-back George Cohen made his Fulham début in a 2–1 home defeat at the hands of Liverpool in March 1957. It was his only appearance that season but midway through the 1957–58 season, Cohen won a regular spot in the Fulham side, helping them to that season's FA Cup semi-final. In 1958–59, he missed just one game as the Cottagers won promotion to the First Division and over the next nine seasons, the speedy full-back missed just a handful of games due to injury. In 1961–62 he helped the club to another FA Cup semi-final before in May 1964 he won the first of 37 caps for England against Uruguay at Wembley. He was in the England side that won the World Cup in 1966, forming a formidable full-back pairing with Ray Wilson and was the last Fulham player to win an England cap! Sadly for Fulham and England, Cohen

George Cohen

received a nasty knee injury in a First Division game against Liverpool in December 1967. Though he tried to make a comeback, the injury virtually ended the career of the Kensington-born defender. Cohen, who had scored six goals in 459 League and Cup games, had a brief spell coaching the juniors at Craven Cottage before leaving to develop his business interests. He won a five-year battle with cancer and now combines his interests in building and property development with raising money for cancer charities.

COLEMAN, CHRIS Swansea-born Chris Coleman joined his home-town club from Manchester City juniors in September 1987 and in his first season with the Swans helped them win promotion to the Third Division via the play-offs. He also won Welsh Cup winners' medals in 1989 and 1991 but after four seasons at the Vetch, in which he appeared in 196 first-team games, he left to join Crystal Palace for a fee of £275,000. At Selhurst Park, Coleman won the first of 24 full caps for Wales when he played against Austria in 1992 and went on to appear in 190 games for the Eagles in a four-year stay with the club. In December 1995 he signed for Blackburn Rovers for £2.8 million and though he took a little time to settle in alongside Colin Hendry in the heart of the Blackburn defence, he improved rapidly as the season progressed. However, in 1996–97 an Achilles tendon injury reduced his number of appearances and when Roy Hodgson became manager at Ewood Park, Coleman did not figure in his plans. After appearing in only 32 games, he was allowed to join Kevin Keegan's Fulham for £2.1 million. In an impressive first season at Craven Cottage, Coleman, who made his début in a 1–1 home draw against Brentford, was voted by his fellow professionals into the PFA award-winning Second Division team. Appointed club captain, he was selected for the PFA side for a second successive year and took his tally of goals to six in 84 games as Fulham won the Second Division Championship.

COLEMAN, TIM Goalscoring forward Tim Coleman began his career with his home-town club Kettering before joining Northampton Town in 1910. One year later he was transferred to Woolwich Arsenal and in his first season at Highbury he broke the club's League goalscoring record with 17 goals in 30 games, a total which included a hat-trick against Burnley. In the club's promotion-winning season of 1903–04, he broke his own record by scoring 23 goals. His consistency was rewarded in February

Chris Coleman

1907 when he was awarded a full England cap against Ireland. Coleman had scored 84 goals in 196 games for the Gunners when in February 1908, with the club suffering financially, he was allowed to join Everton for £700. Whilst at Goodison, he helped the club finish runners-up in the Football League but after three seasons, in which he scored 30 goals in 71 games, he moved to Sunderland. After just one season in the north-east, he joined

Fulham and made his début for the Cottagers in a 1–0 defeat at Bristol City on the opening day of the 1911–12 season. Forming a good understanding with Herbert Pearce, he scored 15 goals in 31 games as Fulham finished eighth in Division Two. In 1912–13, Coleman was the club's leading scorer with 20 goals including hat-tricks in successive wins over Wolves (Home 4–2) and Stockport County (Home 7–0). He had scored 48 goals in 100 games for Fulham before leaving to play for Nottingham Forest. He retired during the First World War but later played non-League football for Tunbridge Wells. He finished his involvement with the game after a coaching spell in Holland.

COLLINS, ARTHUR Leicester-born Arthur Collins began his career with his home-town club, Leicester Fosse, where he was a consistent performer as an elegantly constructive wing-half. He had played in 82 games for Fosse when Fulham manager Harry Bradshaw brought him to Craven Cottage in the summer of 1905. He made his Southern League début in a 1–1 home draw against Millwall Athletic and went on to appear in 63 games over the next two seasons as the Cottagers won the Southern League Championship in both 1905–06 and 1906–07. Dubbed 'Prince Arthur' by the Craven Cottage crowd, he came close to England honours when playing in the 1906 Professionals v Amateurs international trial and by 1909 was on the management committee of the Players Union. Collins went on to play in 197 League games for Fulham, helping them to a best position of fourth in 1907–08, their first season in the Second Division. He left Craven Cottage in 1914 to move back into the Southern League with Norwich City before then returning to play wartime football for Leicester Fosse.

COLOURS Fulham's first colours were a uniform of white shirts and black shorts and these have remained the same with a few variations ever since. The club's present colours are white shirts with a red and black trim, black shorts and white stockings with a red and black trim. Fulham's change colours are lime green shirts with navy trim, navy shorts and navy stockings.

CONEY, DEAN Dagenham-born centre-forward Dean Coney worked his way through the ranks at Craven Cottage before making his League début for Fulham in a 2–1 home win over Newport County in March 1981. After scoring three goals in the remaining six games of the season, he started the 1981–82 campaign as the club's first-choice striker alongside Gordon

Dean Coney

Davies. That season, Fulham won promotion to the Second Division and Coney in his first full season with the club netted 13 goals in 42 games. He struggled to find his goalscoring touch the following season but he returned to win four England Under-21 caps and top the club's scoring charts in 1985–86 with 12 goals. He had taken his tally of goals to 72 in 246 League and Cup games when in the summer of 1987 he moved to Queen's Park Rangers along with Paul Parker. In a little under two seasons at

Loftus Road, Coney scored seven goals in 48 League games before moving to Norwich City where he ended his first-class career.

CONSECUTIVE HOME GAMES Fulham played an extraordinarily intense sequence of four home games in succession in just 13 days (14–26 March 1921)

Date	*Opponents*	*Score*
14 March 1921	Coventry City	Won 2–0
19 March 1921	Nottingham Forest	Won 2–1
25 March 1921	Birmingham	Won 5–0
26 March 1921	Rotherham County	Won 1–0

They also played five League games in succession at Craven Cottage during the 1977–78 season but this was over a period of 56 days.

Date	*Opponents*	*Score*
14 January 1978	Bristol Rovers	Drew 1–1
4 February 1978	Tottenham Hotspur	Drew 1–1
25 February 1978	Crystal Palace	Drew 1–1
7 March 1978	Cardiff City	Won 1–0
10 March 1978	Luton Town	Won 1–0

CONSECUTIVE SCORING – LONGEST SEQUENCE Frank Newton and Bedford Jezzard hold the club record for consecutive scoring, both players being on target in nine consecutive League games. Their records are:

Frank Newton (1932–33)	Bedford Jezzard (1953–54)
Lincoln City (H 3–2) 2 goals	Plymouth Argyle (H 3–1) 3 goals
Burnley (A 3–3) 2 goals	Plymouth Argyle (A 2–2) 1 goal

Bradford (H 5–2) 2 goals	Brentford (H 4–1) 1 goal
Plymouth Argyle (A 3–2) 2 goals	West Ham Utd (H 3–4) 1 goal
Oldham Athletic (H 1–0)1 goal	Leeds United (A 2–1) 1 goal
Manchester Utd (A 3–4) 1 goal	Birmingham (H 5–2) 1 goal
Stoke (H 1–3) 1 goal	Nottingham F (A 1–4) 1 goal
Charlton A (A 2–1) 1 goal	Luton Town (H 5–1) 1 goal
Tottenham H (H 2–2) 1 goal	Derby County (A 3–3) 1 goal

CONROY, MIKE After beginning his career as an apprentice with Coventry City, Glasgow-born forward Mike Conroy returned to Scotland to play for Clydebank. He was top scorer in his four seasons at Kilbowie Park and after leaving for a short spell with St Mirren, he joined Reading in September 1988 for a fee of £40,000. He was used more as a utility player at Elm Park but in the summer of 1991 he moved to Burnley where he was restored to the forward line. He helped the Clarets win the Fourth Division Championship in his first season at Turf Moor, scoring 24 goals in 38 games and 30 in all competitions. Unable to recapture his best form in 1992–93, Conroy, who had scored 46 goals in 109 games joined Preston North End for £85,000. In each of his two seasons at Deepdale, he helped the Lilywhites reach the play-offs but towards the end of his stay, the goals dried up and in August 1995 he signed for Fulham for £75,000. He made his débút in a 4–2 home win over Mansfield Town on the opening day of the 1995–96 season, ending the campaign as the club's leading scorer with 14 League and Cup goals including a hat-trick in a 7–0 rout of Swansea City. When Fulham won promotion in 1996–97, Conroy was again the Cottagers' leading scorer with 23 goals, his performances winning him selection in the PFA divisional team and the supporters' Player of the Year award. A nasty injury the following season, coupled with the arrival of Paul Moody, restricted his first-team appearances and in March 1998, after scoring 42 goals in 115 games, he returned to the north-west to play for Blackpool. Unable to win a regular spot in the Seasiders' team, he has spent two spells on loan at Chester City.

CONWAY, JIMMY Dublin-born midfield player Jimmy Conway

Mike Conroy

was one of a family of 17, winning caps at schoolboy, youth and amateur levels. He began his career with Bohemians but in May 1966 he left to join Fulham. He made his début in a 2–2 draw at Liverpool on 8 October 1966, later that month winning the first of 19 full caps for the Republic of Ireland when he played against Spain in Dublin. Conway was a regular member of the Fulham first-team for ten seasons and in 1969–70, when they finished fourth in Division Two, he scored 21 goals in 46 League games, netting two more in the League Cup. The following season he helped the club win promotion and though he then began to suffer from a series of injuries, he returned to full fitness to help the Cottagers reach the 1975 FA Cup final at Wembley. Conway had scored 76 goals in 360 League and Cup games before in the summer of 1976 following coach Bill Taylor to Manchester City. After just one season at Maine Road, he left the Football League to play in the United States.

COOK, MAURICE An old-fashioned type of centre-forward, Maurice Cook began his Football League career with Watford whom he joined from his home-town club, Berkhamstead. In four and a half seasons at Vicarage Road, Cook, who played in all of the forward positions, scored 84 goals in 215 games before leaving to join Fulham in February 1958. He made his début in a 2–2 home draw against West Ham United, going on to score nine goals in the remaining 15 games of the season, a campaign in which the Cottagers finished fifth in Division Two. When Fulham won promotion to the First Division in 1958–59, Cook netted a hat-trick on the opening day of the season as Stoke City were beaten 6–1 and ended the campaign with 17 goals. During the club's first season in the top-flight, Cook struggled to retain his first-team place but in 1960–61, after reforging the prolific goalscoring partnership with Graham Leggatt, he netted a hat-trick in a 4–2 win at Wolverhampton Wanderers on the final day of the season. Cook was the club's leading scorer in each of the next two seasons, netting hat-tricks in wins over Sheffield United (Home 5–2) in March 1962 and Sheffield Wednesday (Home 4–1) in September 1962. Cook went on to score 97 goals in 248 League and Cup games before moving to Reading where, after just one season with the then Elm Park club, he ended his first-class career.

CRAVEN COTTAGE The Cottage was built in 1780 by Baron Craven in the middle of woods which formed part of Anne Boleyn's old hunting grounds. Money-lender Charles King made it his home, whilst other famous owners were novelist Edward Bulwer-Lytton and Sir Ralph Howard. The Cottage was destroyed by fire in May 1888 and the site became completely overgrown until Fulham's arrival some six years later. They agreed to clear the land and lay out a ground in return for a half share of the gate money. However, it took over two years' preparation before the Cottagers could move in. It was 10

October 1876 before the club played their first match there when they entertained Minerva in the Middlesex Senior Cup. Shortly afterwards, the ground's first stand was built – described as an 'Orange Box Stand', it consisted of four wooden structures, each holding 250 seats and each with its own gabled corrugated iron roof. Fulham fans nicknamed it the 'Rabbit Hutch'. A few years later, London County Council tried to close the Rabbit Hutch on safety grounds. This led to a court case in January 1905 after which Fulham hired Scottish engineer Archibald Leitch to extend Craven Cottage's three banks of terracing and build a new stand and pavilion – a scheme that cost £15,000. The corner pavilion was a first south of the border whilst the stand built on Stevenage Road was the first of a series of Leitch designs which was soon to become a familiar sight at British grounds. Two years after completion, the new Craven Cottage staged the England v Wales international and in 1911 the ground was the venue of a rugby league international between England and Australia. One of Fulham's directors, Henry Norris, was so disappointed that the club hadn't achieved First Division status that he and fellow director William Hall took over at Woolwich Arsenal and tried to merge them with Fulham at Craven Cottage! After this move had failed, very little happened until 1933 when there was talk that the Cottage may be demolished to make way for ground improvements. Thankfully, that didn't materialise and on 8

The Craven Cottage Faithful

October 1938, when the club record gate of 49,335 watched the game against Millwall, the ground had changed little since 1905. In fact, it wasn't until the Cottagers were in the top-flight that any improvements were made. In 1961 the Hammersmith End was extended and the following year Fulham became the last First Division side to erect floodlights. The club also installed a new electronic scoreboard and in 1965 the Hammersmith End was covered. Despite relegation to Division Two, the riverside terracing was cleared to make way for a new stand. Costing £334,000 and housing 4,200 seats, the Riverside Stand (which was later named after Fulham director Eric Miller) was first opened for a friendly against Benfica in February 1972. Miller had used his contacts to get the stand built but in 1977 he was involved in a political and financial scandal and committed suicide. Since then, the struggle for Craven Cottage has dominated the club's affairs. There have been three public enquiries and nine planning applications. The Cottage story is very complex, much too detailed to include in this entry, suffice to say that the club's future plans are to redevelop three sides and purchase the ground!

CRICKETERS There have been a number of Fulham footballers who were also cricketers of real note. During the First World War, Surrey and England captain Percy Fender also kept goal for the Cottagers. His total of 19,034 first-class runs at an average of 26.65 include a 35-minute century at Northampton – one of the classic cricketing feats. Andy Ducat, who both played for and managed Fulham, was a highly talented forcing batsman whose total of 23,108 runs at 38.64 includes scores of 306 not out against Oxford University and 290 not out against Essex. He was a double international who also captained the FA Cup-winning Aston Villa team in 1929. Bob Gregory, who made 37 League appearances for Fulham, was more renowned as a Surrey cricketer than a footballer and in 22 years at the Oval scored 18,978 runs at 34.75 and captured 434 wickets at 31.97 runs apiece. His highest score was 243 against Somerset in 1938. Off-break bowler Henry White appeared in eight championship games for Warwickshire, though it was as a goalscoring centre-forward with Arsenal that he made his name. He could never reproduce this form when he joined Fulham. Jim Hammond was one of the club's most consistent and prolific goalscorers, netting 150 in 342 games. He played county cricket for Sussex, scoring 4,251 runs at 18.73 and taking 428 wickets at 28.71 runs apiece, including a hat-trick against Warwickshire at Hove in 1946.

Johnny Arnold, who represented England at both football and cricket, joined Fulham from Southampton. Arnold, who scored 21,596 runs at 32.92, was a mainstay of Hampshire's batting from 1929 to 1950 – his highest score being 227 against Glamorgan at Cardiff in 1932. Bill Caesar, who made just one League appearance for the Cottagers, had a handful of games for both Somerset and Surrey whilst centre-half Gordon Brice turned out for Northamptonshire in the years just after the Second World War. George Cox junior, as did his father, played for Sussex, scoring 22,687 runs at 32.22 and a best of 234 not out against the Indians in 1946. For Fulham he scored twice on his début but spent most of his career at Craven Cottage in the reserves. He later won fame as a fine after-dinner speaker in his capacity as president of Sussex's Cricket Society.

CROAL, JIMMY Glasgow-born inside-forward Jimmy Croal began his career with Falkirk and at the age of 18 made the first of three full international appearances for Scotland when he played against Ireland in Dublin. With Falkirk, Croal won a Scottish Cup winners' medal when they beat Raith Rovers 2–0 in the 1913 final. At the end of the following season, the balding Croal came south of the border to play for Chelsea. Though his career at Stamford Bridge was interrupted by the First World War, he managed to score 22 goals in 130 League games played before and after the hostilities. He also appeared in the 1915 FA Cup final when the Pensioners lost 3–0 to Sheffield United. In March 1922, Croal joined Fulham, making his début in a 1–0 defeat at Bristol City, though he did score twice on his first appearance at Craven Cottage as South Shields were beaten 3–0. Though Croal remained with the Cottagers for three seasons, scoring six goals in 36 games, he had left his best football behind him. The little Scotsman, who was renowned for his ball control, died by his own hand at the early age of 44.

CUSACK, NICK Former Birmingham Polytechnic student Nick Cusack was playing for Alvechurch when Leicester City signed him in June 1987. Plunged straight into the Foxes' first-team on the opening day of the 1987–88 season, he struggled to win a regular place and, having impressed against Peterborough United in a testimonial game, he joined 'The Posh' in an exchange deal which took Alan Paris to Leicester. After finishing the 1988–89 season as the London Road club's top scorer, he was transferred to Motherwell for £100,000. An instant hit with the Fir Park club, he helped them reach the 1991 Scottish Cup final but, after scoring 23 goals in 86 games, he left to play for Darlington, for a club record fee of £95,000. Unable to prevent the Quakers from being relegated, he was transferred to Oxford United for a similar fee. After a brief loan spell with Wycombe Wanderers, he joined Fulham on a free transfer in November 1994. His first game in Fulham colours came in a 1–0 win at Northampton Town, Cusack ending the season with a hat-trick in a 5–0 defeat of Rochdale on the final day of the campaign. The following season he was switched to central midfield where his performances earned him the club's Player of the Year award, whilst in 1996–97 he moved to play sweeper in a Fulham defence that was the meanest in the Third Division. After helping the club win promotion that season, he was injured in the early part of the 1997–98 campaign and, unable to regain his first-team spot, he left to join Swansea City. Cusack, who had scored 19 goals in 141 games with Fulham, was soon made captain of the Swans and has since proved to be the Vetch Field club's most consistent player.

CUTBUSH, JOHN John Cutbush was born in Malta where his father, Dennis, a former England Amateur international, was stationed with the Royal Navy. After returning to live in England, he represented Kent Schoolboys before joining Tottenham Hotspur. Unable to make the grade at White Hart Lane, he joined Fulham on a free transfer in the summer of 1972, six years after turning professional. After making his Cottagers' début as a substitute for Roger Cross in a 3–1 home defeat by Preston North End, Cutbush made the right-back spot his own for the next five seasons. In 1974–75 he helped the club reach the FA Cup final, winning a runners-up medal as West Ham United beat the Cottagers 2–0. Following the arrival of Peter Storey from Arsenal, Cutbush found his place in the side under threat and, having scored three goals in 160 games, left to play for Sheffield United. He spent a little over four seasons at Bramhall Lane but, following the club's relegation to the Fourth Division in 1980–81, the staunch defender was released.

D

DALRYMPLE, ROBERT Robert Dalrymple began his career playing in the Scottish League for Hearts with whom he won a Scottish Cup runners-up medal in 1903 after they had lost to Rangers in two replays. He then came south to play for Plymouth Argyle before returning to Scottish League action with Rangers. The lure of the south coast again proved a strong attraction and he had a brief spell with Portsmouth before joining Fulham in the summer of 1907. After his début in the 1–0 home defeat by Hull City, the club's first-ever Football League game, he went on to have an outstanding season. The Cottagers, who finished fourth in Division Two and reached the semi-finals of the FA Cup, were indebted to Dalrymple who topped the scoring charts with 22 goals. His total included three League hat-tricks in the wins over Lincoln City (away 4–2) Gainsborough Trinity (home 6–0) and Clapton Orient (home 4–0). Forming a prolific striking partnership with Fred Harrison, Dalrymple continued to find the net in 1908–9 but then his scoring rate began to fall away. He had scored 44 goals in 108 games when he was transferred to Clapton Orient in January 1911. Dalrymple was almost 40 when he played the last of his 139 games, having scored 37 goals for the Millfields Road club.

DAVIES, GORDON Fulham's greatest-ever goalscorer, Gordon Davies began his career with Manchester City, joining the Maine Road club as an apprentice in 1972. Failing to make the grade, he decided to train to become a teacher whilst playing non-League football for his home-town team of Merthyr Tydfil. In March

1978, Fulham manager Bobby Campbell paid £4,000 for his services and he made his début as a substitute for Mark Lovell in a 2–0 home defeat by Mansfield Town. After that, Davies was an automatic choice and in 1979–80 he topped the club's scoring charts for the first time. His total of 15 goals in 39 games included hat-tricks in the games against Birmingham City (away 4–3) and Leicester City (away 3–3). Not surprisingly, his prolific goalscoring attracted the national selectors and in 1980 he won the first of 16 Welsh caps in the game against Turkey. Davies was Fulham's leading scorer for the next four seasons, helping the club win promotion to the Second Division in 1981–82 when he netted 24 goals in 41 games. His next hat-tricks came in the 1983–84 season when he scored four of the goals in a 5–1 rout of Manchester City and all three in the 5–3 home defeat by Chelsea. In November 1984 Chelsea gave Davies the opportunity to prove himself in the First Division but, despite scoring a hat-trick in the 4–3 win at Everton, most of his stay at Stamford Bridge was as understudy to David Speedie. In October 1985 he left to play for Manchester City and, after scoring nine goals in 31 games, he rejoined Fulham. He took his tally of goals in two spells with the club to 178 in 448 League and Cup games before ending his first-class career with Wrexham. Davies later managed Tornado of Norway.

DEATH 'Sonny' Gibbon, who played his early football for Aberdare Athletic and Merthyr Town, joined Fulham in March 1929. He quickly established himself at full-back and won a Third Division (South) Championship medal in 1931–32. Tragically killed in a motor-cycle accident near Deal, Kent on 8 April 1935, his death came as a great shock to everyone connected with Craven Cottage.

DEBUTS 'Tosh' Chamberlain scored with his first kick in the first minute of his League début for Fulham on 20 November 1954 when the Cottagers beat Lincoln City at home 3–2. Ronnie Rooke and Doug McGibbon both scored hat-tricks on their League débuts whilst Harry Hampton did so as a 'guest' during the First World War.

DEFEATS – FEWEST During the 1998–99 season, the Cottagers went through the 46-match programme and suffered only seven defeats in winning the Second Division Championship.

DEFEATS – MOST Fulham's total of 26 defeats during the 1985–86 season is the worst in the club's history.

Gordon Davies

DEFEATS – WORST Fulham's record defeat was the 10–0 thrashing inflicted upon them by Liverpool in a Football League Cup second-round first-leg tie at Anfield on 23 September 1986. The club's worst defeat in the league – 9–0 – was delivered by Wolverhampton Wanderers on 16 September 1959.

DEFENSIVE RECORD Fulham's best defensive record was

established in 1922–23 when the club finished tenth in Division Two. They conceded just 32 goals in that campaign with goalkeeper Arthur Reynolds keeping 18 clean sheets. The club equalled this achievement in 1998–99 in winning the Second Division Championship. Fulham's worst defensive record was in 1967–68 when they conceded 98 goals in finishing bottom of the First Division.

DEMPSEY, JOHN Republic of Ireland international John Dempsey joined Fulham straight from school and, after working his way up through the ranks, he made his League début in a 2–1 home defeat at the hands of Chelsea in January 1965. The following season, the powerful defender had a brief spell up front and scored a hat-trick in a 5–0 League Cup win over Northampton Town. An ever-present in 1966–67, he scored eight goals in 171 games and in January 1969 was allowed to join Chelsea for £70,000. During his three and a half seasons at Stamford Bridge, Dempsey played in three major cup finals. He won an FA Cup winners' medal in 1970, a European Cup Winners' Cup medal in 1971, having scored with a superb volley, and a League Cup runners-up medal in 1972. In August 1972 he suffered the first of the catalogue of serious injuries which were to blight the remainder of his career. He went on to score seven goals in 207 games for Chelsea before taking the well-trodden path to America in March 1978 where he played for Philadelphia Furies.

DICKS, ALAN Alan Dicks made only one appearance for Chelsea during their League Championship-winning season of 1954–55 but worked hard and took an interest in all aspects of the game. He was only 23 when he obtained a coaching badge, later becoming assistant manager to Jimmy Hill at Coventry City as the Sky Blues went from the Third to the First Division. In the wake of Hill's resignation, Dicks left to become manager of Bristol City. After reaching the League Cup semi-finals in 1971, the Robins won promotion to the First Division in 1975–76 and during the four years they were in the top-flight, Dicks became the longest-serving manager in the Football League. He left Ashton Gate in 1980 when the club was relegated and, after a season in Greek soccer, returned to the English game as assistant manager to Ray Lewington at Fulham. In the summer of 1990, they reversed roles but, midway through the following season, he lost full control of team affairs when Jimmy Hill took on a more active role. He was later sacked after a run of poor results.

DISMISSALS The player with the unenviable distinction of being the first to be given his marching orders in a League match is winger Willie Walker who was dismissed in a 3–2 win at Bradford on 15 February 1913.

Bill Dodgin (Senior)

DODGIN, BILL (Senior) Having started his playing career with Huddersfield Town, Bill Dodgin moved to Lincoln City before joining Charlton Athletic, a side he helped elevate from the Third to the First Division in the space of two seasons. Curiously, he left the Valley for Bristol Rovers before he could taste top-flight football. After leaving Eastville, he played for Clapton Orient before arriving at The Dell in the close season of 1939, the 1939–40 season having been abandoned. Dodgin was destined never to play League football again. In 1946 he was appointed team manager of Southampton. Twice it looked as if the Saints would gain promotion to the First Division but twice they blew it, finishing third in 1947–48 and again in April 1949 after leading the Second Division table by eight points. An attractive offer lured Dodgin to Craven Cottage in the summer of 1949 as Fulham embarked on their first season in the top-flight after winning the Second Division Championship the previous season. The Cottagers spent three seasons in Division One before relegation in 1951–52 and though Dodgin was responsible for discovering Johnny Haynes, he failed to return the club to the top-flight and, in October 1953, he was sacked. He had a short spell with Brentford and coached in Italy before taking charge at Yiewsley. He later managed Bristol Rovers and produced a number of attacking sides before retiring from the game.

DODGIN, BILL (Junior) Bill Dodgin was playing for Southampton junior team as an amateur but when his father, who was the Saints manager, left to take charge of Fulham, he followed him to Craven Cottage. After two years' National Service, Dodgin junior made his League début in a 1–0 win at Preston North End in December 1951, going on to appear in 36 games before being transferred to Arsenal for £8,000 a year later. With the Gunners, he won an England Under-23 cap against Italy in January 1954. Despite losing his club place the following season when his form deserted him, he returned to play in 208 games before being given a free transfer back to Fulham in March 1961. He played in the Cottagers' FA Cup semi-final defeat by Burnley in 1962 but a broken leg in the match at Aston Villa some seven months later virtually ended his playing career. Dodgin, who played in 113 games for Fulham during his two spells with the club, turned to coaching and management. After a short spell with Millwall he took charge of Queen's Park Rangers and led the Loftus Road club from the Third to the First Division and to a League Cup final victory in 1967. In December 1968 he was appointed manager of Fulham but was unable to prevent the club slipping into the Third Division. However, within two seasons he had built a team that won promotion, only missing the championship after losing 1–0 at home to Preston North End.

Unfortunately the club floundered in the Second Division and a year later he was sacked. In 1976 he led Northampton Town to promotion to Division Three and did the same for Brentford two years later. He managed the Cobblers for a second time but after the club had to seek re-election he was sacked.

DRAWS Fulham played their greatest number of drawn League matches in a single season in 1986–87, 1992–93 and 1995–96 when 17 of their matches ended all square. Their fewest was in 1956–57 when only four of their matches were drawn. The club's highest scoring draw was 5–5 in two away matches, the first against Coventry City (2 January 1932) in the League and then against Grimsby Town (9 January 1954) in the FA Cup.

DUCAT, ANDY A sporting legend at the turn of the twentieth century, Andy Ducat was one of that privileged few who have played both football and cricket for England. He began his footballing career in junior football with Westcliffe Athletic before joining local League side Southend United in 1903. He moved on to Woolwich Arsenal in January 1905, becoming an automatic first-team choice in 1908–09. The following season he won the first of his six full caps and went on to score 21 goals in 188 League and Cup games before a £1,000 offer from Aston Villa was accepted by the Gunners. His Villa career got off to a disastrous start when he broke a leg at Maine Road in September 1912. As a result, he missed the 1913 FA Cup final. However, when Jimmy Harrop was injured in 1920, Ducat took over and captained Villa to victory in the FA Cup final over Huddersfield Town. He left Villa Park in May 1921 to join Fulham and to be near his beloved Surrey Cricket Club for whom he scored 23,108 runs between 1906 and 1931. Ducat made the first of 69 appearances for the Cottagers in a 2–0 defeat at Coventry in the third game of the 1921–22 season. Taking over as club captain, he played his last game in March 1924 before replacing Phil Kelso as manager. Though he was a great favourite with the Fulham crowd as a player, his two seasons as manager were unhappy ones. In fact, in 1925–26 the club only survived relegation to the Third Division (South) by beating Bradford City 2–0 in the final game of the season. The first Fulham manager to be sacked, Ducat collapsed and died in July 1942 – on the square, bat in hand – whilst playing for Surrey Home Guard against Sussex Home Guard at Lord's.

DUNNE, JIMMY Dublin-born central defender Jimmy Dunne began his career with Shelbourne Rovers before he was snapped up by Millwall following a series of impressive displays. Despite rave reviews in the club's reserve side, he was never given a chance in the first-team and in July 1967 he joined Torquay United. After three seasons at Plainmoor, manager Bill Dodgin junior paid £15,000 to bring Dunne to Craven Cottage. He made his début in a 1–0 win at Barnsley on the opening day of the 1970–71 season, going on to miss only one game of a campaign in which the club won promotion to the Second Division. He scored twice: in his first home game, a 4–1 victory over Swansea, and a last-minute equaliser at Preston North End to secure an important point. His performances led to his being capped by the Republic of Ireland against Austria in 1971, after which he was a first-team regular for Fulham until 1974. Dunne, who had scored two goals in 166 games, decided to emigrate to South Africa but, when things didn't work out, he returned to Craven Cottage for a brief spell, playing in the reserves before rejoining Torquay United where he took his tally of League games in his two spells to 247.

DWIGHT, ROY The uncle of rock star Elton John, Roy Dwight began his career with non-League Hastings United before joining Fulham in the summer of 1950. However, it was almost five years before he made his first-team début as the Cottagers won 4–1 at Ipswich Town in March 1955. Over the next two seasons, Dwight scored seven goals in eight games but still couldn't force his way into the side on a regular basis because of the form of Bedford Jezzard. When injury forced the star Fulham striker to retire, Dwight came into the side and in 1956–57 scored in each of the opening seven games of the season including a hat-trick in the 7–3 home defeat of Swansea Town. He went on to be the club's top scorer with 25 goals in 34 games including further hat-tricks in the wins over Notts County (home 5–1), Port Vale (home 6–3) and Swansea Town again (away 5–4). In 1957–58 he helped the club reach the semi-final of the FA Cup where they lost 5–3 to Manchester United in a replay. He top-scored again, his total of 22 goals in 30 outings including four in a 6–3 home win over Sheffield United. In July 1958, after scoring 57 goals in 80 games, he joined Nottingham Forest for £6,000. At the end of his first season, he appeared for Forest in the FA Cup final and scored against Luton Town before breaking his leg later in the game. After two seasons out of the game, he played non-League football for Gravesend and Northfleet before returning to League action with Coventry City. After a brief spell with Millwall, Roy Dwight managed Tooting and Mitcham and was in charge when they embarked on their famous FA Cup runs.

E

EARLE, STEVE A prolific scorer for Fulham, Steve Earle made his Cottagers début in a 2–0 defeat at Nottingham Forest in February 1964 before scoring on his home début the following week against Blackpool. However, it was midway through the 1965–66 season before he established himself in the Fulham side, following the appointment of Dave Sexton as coach. Earle netted 11 goals in 15 games including a hat-trick against Northampton Town (away 4–2) to help the club pull clear of the First Division relegation zone. Earle was then a virtual ever-present in the Fulham side for the next eight seasons, topping the scoring chart in 1969–70, 1971–72 and 1972–73. His best season was 1969–70 when his total of 23 included five goals in the 8–0 defeat of Halifax Town and a hat-trick against Stockport County (away 4–1). He went on to score 108 goals in 327 League and Cup games before leaving Craven Cottage to join Leicester City for £100,000 in November 1973. Having helped the Foxes dispose of his former club on the way to the 1974 FA Cup semi-final, the unselfish front runner suffered something of a goal drought before rediscovering his shooting boots. Earle, who took a belated Craven Cottage testimonial in October 1975, later played in the NASL for Detroit Express, Tulsa Roughnecks and Wichita.

EARLY GROUNDS Fulham St Andrew's first played on wasteland on Star Road close to the church but after four years they moved to Eelbrook Common. From 1883 to 1888, the club played on a

Steve Earle

variety of grounds, including Lillie Road, Putney Lower Common and Ranelagh House. In 1888 they played across the river from Craven Cottage at Barn Elms before returning to play at Eelbrook Common. Three years later the club found its first enclosed ground, shared with Wasps Rugby Club, at the Half Moon pub on the Lower Richmond Road. They then shared Captain James' Field on Halford Road with their great rivals of those early days, Stanley FC, for a year before moving to Craven Cottage in 1896.

Jeff Eckhardt

ECKHARDT, JEFF Utility player Jeff Eckhardt began his Football League career with his home-town club Sheffield United, making 83 appearances before moving to Fulham in November 1987 for a fee of £50,000. He made his début in a 2–0 win at Rotherham United and held his place for the rest of that 1987–88 campaign, playing in the remaining 29 matches and scoring his first goal for the club in a 3–1 home win over Southend United towards the end of the season. Able to play at the back, in midfield or up front, Eckhardt missed very few games over the next seven seasons and had appeared in 268 League and Cup games, scoring 25 goals when, in July 1994, he was transferred to Stockport County for £50,000. He spent two seasons at Edgeley Park, scoring 12 goals in 75 games before a £30,000 fee took him to Cardiff City. Now in his fourth season at Ninian Park, Eckhardt has scored 15 goals in 102 games for the Bluebirds having helped them win promotion to the Second Division in 1998–99.

EDELSTON, JOE Joe Edelston played for Hull City and

Manchester City before joining Fulham in November 1920. He made his début in a 3–0 defeat at Sheffield Wednesday and though he was coming to the end of his career, he completed an impressive half-back line alongside Andy Ducat and Jimmy Torrance. He had appeared in 71 games for the Cottagers when, in 1925, he was made captain and coach of the club's reserve team. He kept this position for twelve years, during which time he served under six different managers. He also acted as the club's caretaker-manager on two occasions, the second of these after Jimmy Hogan had been dismissed. It was assumed that Edeleston, a qualified FA coach, would be appointed on a permanent basis but the Fulham board opted for Jack Peart instead. Unfortunately for the Cottagers, the two men fell out, and Edelston, whose reserve side were top of the Combination, was accused of countermanding Peart's tactical instruction. Edelston was asked to leave and after a spell coaching Brentford was appointed manager of Reading before ending his involvement with the game as assistant manager of Leyton Orient.

EDMONDS, GEORGE A centre-forward in the old-fashioned mode, George Edmonds joined Watford as a professional in 1912 and in 1914–15 helped them win the Southern League Championship. Whilst with Watford he played for England in a Victory International but in June 1920 he moved to Wolverhampton Wanderers for a fee of £1,500. After making his début against Fulham, he went on to end the 1920–21 campaign as the club's leading scorer and played in the FA Cup final against Spurs. Edmonds was Wolves' leading scorer in each of his three full seasons with the club, netting his only hat-trick in April 1923 in the 3–0 victory over Port Vale. After Wolves were relegated in 1922–23, Edmonds became unsettled and wanted to leave Molineux. In September 1923, after scoring 42 goals in 126 games, he moved to Fulham and made his début for the Cottagers in a 1–1 home draw against Bristol City. Though he only played in 23 games that season, Edmonds was the club's leading scorer with 13 goals, including a hat-trick in a 3–1 win over Manchester United. Injuries hampered his progress over the next couple of seasons and in the summer of 1926, after scoring 26 goals in 73 games, he rejoined Watford. He had just one season at Vicarage Road before hanging up his boots.

EVANS, JAMES Merthyr-born half-back James Evans was working down the pit when his home-town team gave him the chance of a career in football. After a number of impressive performances, he

Ray Evans

was transferred to Hereford United in the Midland League. First Division Arsenal signed him but loaned him to their nursery club Margate, who played in the Southern League. During the 1935–36 season, Margate had a fine run in the FA Cup, beating Crystal Palace in the first-round, a match in which Evans scored a hat-trick. Recalled to Highbury, he still couldn't force his way into the Gunners' first-team and, in the summer of 1937, he joined Fulham on a free transfer. Evans made his League début for the Cottagers in a 4–0 defeat at Plymouth Argyle on the opening day of the 1937–38 season. He missed very few games in the two seasons leading up to the outbreak of the Second World War, scoring five goals in 74 League and Cup games. He continued to play for Fulham throughout the war years, appearing in 90 games before retiring prior to the resumption of League football.

EVANS, RAY England Youth international Ray Evans began his Football League career with Tottenham Hotspur where he was unfortunate not to win any major honours. Evans always seemed to lose out to the more experienced Joe Kinnear when the big games came round. He was dropped for the 1971–72 UEFA Cup clashes with AC Milan and missed the League Cup final of 1973 after playing in most of the earlier rounds. When Terry Neill became manager there seemed to be no place for Evans in the Spurs set-up and in January 1975 he left to join Millwall for £35,000. He spent two years at The Den, making 91 appearances before moving on to Fulham. The attacking full-back made his début for the Cottagers in a 1–1 draw at home to Southampton in March 1977 and over the next three seasons was a first-team regular. He appeared in 89 games, with three of his six goals coming in consecutive games midway through the 1977–78 season. In 1977 he had his first summer spell in America where he played for St Louis Stars. He played for California Surf the following summer then joined Stoke City and finished his British career with the Potters, although he did played for Seattle Sounders in 1982 and 1983. He finished his career in the American Indoor Soccer League before turning to coaching youngsters in the Seattle area.

EVANSON, JOHN Midfielder John Evanson was playing non-League football for Towcester when Oxford United signed him as an amateur in the summer of 1964. Despite making his League début against Bournemouth in 1966, it was 1970–71 before he established himself as a regular member of the Us' side. He had played in 160 games for the Manor Ground club when Blackpool paid £40,000 to secure his services in February 1974. Evanson was an important member of the Seasiders for two seasons but, after being given a free transfer, he left Bloomfield Road to play summer soccer for Miami Toros. It was from there that Fulham manager Bobby Campbell signed Evanson in July 1977. He made his Cottagers' début as a substitute for John Dowie in a 3–1

John Evanson

defeat at Burnley in the second game of the 1976–77 season. Evanson, who stayed at Craven Cottage for three seasons, played all his football for Fulham in the Second Division and scored five goals in 107 games before joining Bournemouth for £20,000 in the summer of 1979. He played in 53 games for the Dean Court club before leaving to play non-League football for nearby Poole Town.

EVER-PRESENTS Fifty-seven Fulham players have been ever-present in a League season. The greatest number is four, a record held by Arthur Reynolds and Syd Gibbons.

F

FA CUP The club's first game in the FA Cup took place on 31 October 1896 when they lost 5–0 at Swanscombe in a second qualifying round match. After reaching the quarter-finals of the competition in 1904–05, where they lost 5–0 at Aston Villa, the Cottagers went one better in 1907–08, their first season of League football, when they reached the semi-finals. After beating Luton Town (home 8–3) and Norwich City (away 2–1), the Cottagers beat two First Division clubs in Manchester City (home 3–1 after a 1–1 draw) and Manchester United (home 2–1). In the semi-final, Fulham played Newcastle United at Anfield but their hopes of reaching the final were dashed when they went three goals down in the first five minutes. Later they lost goalkeeper Leslie Skene through injury and ended up losing 6–0, still the highest recorded score at this stage of the competition. In 1911–12, Fulham reached the quarter-finals where they lost 3–0 at West Bromwich Albion but in getting there had the satisfaction of beating First Division Liverpool 3–0. It was 1925–26 before the Cottagers again reached this stage of the competition, beating three First Division sides – Everton, Liverpool and Notts County – before losing 2–1 at home to Manchester United. Fulham reached the semi-finals again in 1935–36. After beating Brighton (home 2–1) and Blackpool (home 5–2) – a match in which Eddie Perry scored four goals – Fulham eliminated First Division opposition in Chelsea (home 3–2 after a goalless draw) and Derby County (home 3–0). In the semi-final, Fulham's opponents were Sheffield United, also from the Second Division, but in a disappointing game at Molineux the Blades won 2–1. In the FA Cup of 1945–46, the competition was played on a return-leg basis for the only time in its history. In the third-round the Cottagers met Charlton Athletic. In the first leg at the Valley, the Addicks won 3–1 but Fulham beat them 2–1 at Craven Cottage. Charlton went through 4–3 on aggregate, eventually reaching the final where they lost to Derby County. In doing so, they became the only club ever to reach the FA Cup final after losing a match in an earlier round. The Cottagers reached the quarter-finals again in 1947–48, beating Doncaster Rovers (home 2–0), Bristol Rovers (home 5–2) and First Division Everton (away 1–0 after a 1–1 draw) before losing 2–0 at home to Blackpool. Victories over Sheffield Wednesday (home 1–0) Millwall (away 1–0) and Chelsea (home 3–0 after a 1–1 draw) saw the club reach the quarter-finals again in 1950–51 but again the Cottagers were knocked out by Blackpool, who won 1–0 in a closely fought game at Bloomfield Road. In 1957–58, the club not only just missed out on promotion to the First Division but reached the semi-finals of the FA Cup. Wins over Yeovil (home 4–0) Charlton Athletic (away 2–0 after a 1–1 draw), West Ham United (away 3–2) and Bristol Rovers (home 3–1) saw Fulham play Manchester United in the semi-final at Villa Park. In a memorable game, goals from Stevens and Hill gave Fulham a 2–2 draw, necessitating a replay at Highbury four days later. But Tony Macedo had a disappointing game and what many reckon to have been a perfectly good Fulham goal was disallowed. The Cottagers lost 5–3. Fulham reached the semi-final for a fourth time in 1961–62, beating Hartlepool United (home 3–1), Walsall (away 2–0 after a 2–2 draw) and Blackburn Rovers (away 1–0 after a 2–2 draw). Their opponents at Villa Park were Burnley but the game, in which the Cottagers were denied a blatant penalty, ended all-square at 1–1. In the replay at Filbert Street, the Clarets won 2–1. In 1974–75, Fulham, then a Second Division club, at last reached the FA Cup final. All their victories came in away matches: Hull City (1–0 after 1–1 and 2–2 draws), Nottingham Forest (2–1), Carlisle United (1–0) and Birmingham City (1–0 in a semi-final replay after the first meeting at Hillsborough had finished 1–1). In the final, the Cottagers lost 2–0 to West Ham United. Since then, Fulham's best performance came in 1998–99 when they reached the fifth-round before losing 1–0 (away) to Manchester United.

FA CUP FINAL Fulham's one appearance in an FA Cup final came in 1974–75, but their path to only the second all-London final had been less than smooth. The Second Division side's road to the Twin Towers was the longest of any previous finalist – 11 matches. The Cottagers needed seven games to eliminate fellow Second Division clubs Hull City and Nottingham Forest, whilst in the semi-final replay against Birmingham City, John Mitchell scored the game's only goal with just nine seconds remaining. Fulham's opponents in the final were West Ham United, who had last won the FA Cup in 1964, under their captain, Bobby Moore. Now he was in the Fulham side, partnered by another former England international, Alan Mullery. However, it was former Rochdale striker Alan Taylor who burst the Cottagers' bubble, scoring twice in the space of five minutes. The Fulham side comprised: P. Mellor, J. Cutbush, J. Fraser, A. Mullery, J. Lacy, B. Moore, J. Mitchell, J. Conway, V. Busby, A. Slough and L. Barrett.

FANS Perhaps the club's most devoted fan was Yorky Whiting, a dustman from Devon, who not only vowed to leave everything he had to the Cottagers in his will, but also painted his house, named Craven Cottage, in Fulham's colours. A set of goalposts stood at the entrance to his garage whilst most of the inside of his house was decorated with hundreds of the Cottagers' programmes.

FATHER AND SON The club's first full-time manager Harry Bradshaw led the Cottagers to two Southern League titles before they were admitted to the Football League in 1907. In their first season in the competition, Bradshaw helped Fulham finish fourth in Division Two and reach the semi-finals of the FA Cup. His son Joe, who played in six games for Fulham, later returned to Craven Cottage to manage the club but, in his second season in charge, the Cottagers were relegated to the Third Division (South) for the first time in their history. Joe Edelston began his career with Hull City and later played for Manchester City before joining Fulham in November 1920. He made 71 appearances for the Cottagers before spending 12 seasons as captain and coach of the Reserves. Twice he served Fulham as caretaker manager but was never given complete control of club affairs. His son Maurice, who played in Britain's Olympic team and won nine amateur caps and five wartime caps, made three League appearances for the Cottagers. When Joe Edelston left the club after being accused of countermanding Jack Peart's tactical instructions, he took Maurice, later a successful BBC commentator, with him. Bill Dodgin Sr played for Huddersfield Town, Lincoln City and Charlton Athletic before moving to Southampton where he ended his playing days and began his managerial career. In 1949 he moved to Craven Cottage to manage Fulham and Bill Jr followed him shortly afterwards. Bill Dodgin Sr led Fulham to the sixth round of the FA Cup in 1950–51 and signed youngsters Johnny Haynes and Bobby Robson. However, when the club was relegated in 1951–52 and failed to win promotion at the first attempt, Dodgin Sr parted company with the Cottagers. Bill Dodgin Jr appeared in 36 games for the club before leaving to play for Arsenal. He later returned to Craven Cottage and took his total of appearances to 113 before a broken leg virtually ended his playing career. On hanging up his boots, he turned to coaching and management and in 1968 he took charge of the Cottagers. Within two seasons, he had led the club to promotion but after a campaign in which the club just clung on to its Second Division status, he lost his job.

FINCH, JACK Jack Finch was playing for Isthmian League club Walthamstow Avenue when his work as a coach driver took him to Lowestoft. He spent two years playing for the local side and by the time he returned to play for Walthamstow he had built up a fine reputation as a free-scoring forward. A number of clubs were after his signature but Fulham won the race and, in November 1930, Finch joined the Cottagers. He made his début the following month in a 1–0 home defeat at the hands of Brighton and Hove Albion. He went on to make 18 appearances that season, scoring his first goal for the club in a 6–1 home win over Swindon Town on Boxing Day. When Fulham won the Third Division (South) Championship in 1931–32, Finch scored 11 goals, in 39 games as well as creating numerous chances for Newton and Hammond. Following the signing of Johnny Arnold from Southampton, Finch switched to the right-wing. His superb dribbling skill and accurate crosses allied to his devastating speed made him the perfect choice for a wide man, though this versatile player did appear in all the forward positions. When the Second World War broke out, Finch, who scored 51 goals in 295 League and Cup games, was Fulham's longest-serving player. He went on to appear in 79 wartime games, scoring 11 goals, but by the time League football resumed in 1946–47 he had hung up his boots.

FIRST DIVISION The Cottagers have had three spells in the First Division. Their first began in 1949–50 after the club had won the Second Division Championship the previous season. For two seasons they struggled to avoid the drop, the club eventually being relegated in 1951–52. Fulham won promotion to the First Division again in 1958–59. In their first season back, the club finished tenth and this remains the Cottagers' highest-ever position in the Football League. The club's third spell in the 'new' First Division began in 1999–2000 after the club had won the Second Division title with 101 points.

FIRST LEAGUE MATCH Fulham's first Football League match saw them entertain Hull City at Craven Cottage on Tuesday afternoon, 3 September 1907. Despite having most of the play, Fulham lost to the Tigers 1–0. The Fulham team that day was: L. Skene, H. Ross, A. Lindsay, A. Collins, W. Morrison, W. Goldie, R. Dalrymple, W. Freeman, F. Bevan, A. Hubbard and F. Threlfall.

FLEMING, TOM Glasgow-born defender Tom Fleming began his career with non-League Shettleston before joining Dundee. In each of the two seasons Fleming played for the Dens Park club, they finished fourth in the Scottish League, his performances almost leading to his winning full international honours for Scotland. Fleming joined Fulham in January 1922 and manager Phil Kelso gave him his League début straight away: the Cottagers beat Wolves 1–0. Forming a formidable full-back pairing with Alec Chaplin, Fleming was a virtual ever-present for the next three and a half seasons. Though he never scored for the Cottagers, his long-range passes produced a number of goalscoring opportunities for the likes of Barney Travers, George Edmonds and Bill Prouse. He had appeared in 114 League and Cup games when, in October 1925, he left, along with Jimmy Riddell, to end his first-class career with Wigan Borough.

FLOODLIGHTS Fulham was the last First Division club to install floodlights and these were first used for the visit of Sheffield Wednesday in a First Division match on 19 September 1962. A crowd of 22,635 saw Fulham win 4–1; Maurice Cook scored a hat-trick.

FOOTBALL LEAGUE CUP When the Football League Cup was introduced in 1960–61, the Cottagers were one of the First Division clubs to enter the competition. They played their first-ever match in the League Cup on 26 September 1960 but, despite a Maurice Cook goal early in the game, their opponents Bristol Rovers came back to win 2–1. In 1967–68, the club reached the quarter-finals of the League Cup for the first time, beating Tranmere Rovers (home 1–0), Workington (home 6–2 after a 2–2 draw) and Manchester City (home 3–2) to set up a meeting with Huddersfield Town. The Cottagers were held to a 1–1 draw at home before losing 2–1 at Leeds Road. In the win over Workington, Allan Clarke scored four of the club's goals. Fulham reached this stage of the competition for a second time in 1970–71 after beating Orient (home 1–0), Darlington (away 4–0), Queen's Park Rangers (home 2–0) and Swindon Town (home 1–0). In the quarter-finals they lost 1–0 at Bristol City after a goalless draw at Craven Cottage. Over the next few seasons, Fulham struggled to make much headway in the competition, though Steve Earle netted a hat-trick in a 4–0 win over Cambridge United in 1971–72. In 1986–87 the Cottagers suffered their heaviest-ever defeat in the competition when they went down 10–0 at Anfield in the first leg of the second-round tie against Liverpool.

FOOTBALLER OF THE YEAR The Football Writers' Association award for the Footballer of the Year has been won by only one Fulham player: Alan Mullery for 1974–75.

FOUNDATION Churchgoers were responsible for the foundation of Fulham which began life as Fulham St Andrew's Church Sunday School FC in 1879. They went on to win the West London Amateur Cup in 1887 and the West London League title in 1893. The name Fulham had been adopted in 1888, ten years before the club finally went professional.

FRASER, ALEX Inverness-born forward Alex Fraser began his career with his home-town club, Inverness Thistle, before joining Newcastle United in 1902. However, despite a series of impressive displays for the Magpies' reserve side, he couldn't win a place in the first-team and in October 1904 he joined Fulham. He made his Southern League début for the Cottagers in a goalless draw at West Ham United, ending the season with eight goals in 21 games – a total which included five in the 12–0 rout of Wellingborough. Fraser, who continued to find the net with great regularity, won two Southern League Championship medals in 1905–6 and 1906–7. He made his Football League début for Fulham against Chesterfield in October 1907, scoring one of the goals in a 5–0 win. Despite scoring five goals in ten games, he lost his place to Fred Harrison who had joined the club from Southampton. Fraser scored 28 goals in 91 games for Fulham before moving to Bradford Park Avenue and later Darlington and Middlesbrough where injury forced him into premature retirement.

FREEMAN, HARRY Long-serving full-back Harry Freeman made his Fulham début in a 1–1 home draw against Newcastle United in March 1939, his only appearance before the outbreak of the Second World War. During the hostilities he served in the Royal Fusiliers but still appeared in 111 wartime games for the Cottagers. When League football resumed in 1946–47, Freeman and Jim Taylor were the only ever-presents in the Fulham side. Forming an outstanding full-back partnership with Joe Bacuzzi, he was unlucky not to win international recognition, though he did tour Spain and Canada with the FA. Strong in the tackle and possessed of a powerful shot, Freeman loved to join the attack and scored some spectacular goals. One of these, in the FA Cup against Charlton Athletic, so delighted the usually unemotional Freeman that he performed a handstand in the centre circle. Freeman had scored seven goals in 190 games when he left Craven Cottage in October 1952 to play for Walsall. After just one season with the Saddlers, for whom he made 21 appearances, he decided to hang up his boots. He did return to Craven Cottage shortly afterwards to work on the ground-staff before later working in the bakery trade.

FREIGHT ROVER TROPHY A competition designed solely and specifically for Associate Members of the Football League, the Freight Rover Trophy replaced the original Associate Members' Cup for the 1984–85 season. Fulham first participated in the competition in 1986–87, beating Cambridge United 4–0 at the Abbey Stadium in their first match. Despite losing 2–1 at home to Southend United in their other group match, the Cottagers qualified for the knockout stages and beat Northampton Town 3–2 in the first-round, courtesy of goals by Achampong, Barnett and Marshall. In the second-round, Fulham were involved in a remarkable game with Aldershot at the Recreation Ground. After drawing 1–1 at the end of extra-time, the game went to penalties which the Shots won 11–10.

FRYER, JACK Goalkeeper Jack Fryer played his early football for Abbey Rovers and Cromford before joining Derby County in the summer of 1897. One of the game's most imposing keepers, standing 6ft 3ins tall and weighing almost 14 stone, Fryer appeared in three FA Cup finals for the Rams, on each occasion on the losing side. His last appearance in a final, when Bury beat the Rams 6–0 in 1903, proved also to be the last of his 199 first-team appearances for the club. Fryer was clearly unfit and had conceded three goals. The club decided to try someone else.

Fryer joined Fulham in June 1903 and made his début in a goalless draw at home to Spurs on the opening day of the 1903–4 season. Fryer won the first of two Southern League Championship medals in 1905–6, keeping 18 clean sheets in 30 games. The following season he kept 19 clean sheets in 36 games as the Cottagers retained the title. After receiving a particularly nasty injury towards the end of the 1906–7 season, he didn't play at all in the following campaign and made just 19 Football League appearances before being forced to retire in 1910. Fryer, who had played in a total of 170 games for the Cottagers, ran a pub near Stamford Bridge for a number of years.

FULL MEMBERS CUP Fulham first entered the Full Members Cup, so called because it was originally open only to First and Second Division clubs, in 1985–86 but, after drawing 0–0 at Shrewsbury Town, and losing at home 2–0 to Oxford United, they went out of the competition without scoring a goal.

G

GALE, TONY When the legendary Bobby Moore retired at the end of the 1976–77 season, 16–year-old England Youth international Tony Gale, not yet a professional, took his place at the heart of Fulham's defence. Having made his début in a 1–1 draw at Charlton Athletic on the opening day of the 1977–78 season, Gale became a Fulham regular for seven seasons, helping them win promotion to the Second Division in 1981–82, a season in which he won an England Under-21 cap against Poland. He had scored 21 goals in 318 games when he joined West Ham United for a fee of £225,000 in the summer of 1984. He soon settled into the Hammers' team, forming a formidable partnership with Alvin Martin and in 1985–86, when West Ham United finished third in Division One, he played in all 51 League and Cup games. He also played in the FA Cup semi-final of 1991 against Nottingham Forest and, controversially, was sent off after 26 minutes of the match. Gale appeared in 368 first-team games before leaving Upton Park to play for Blackburn Rovers. His stay at Ewood Park was brief and in September 1995 he joined Crystal Palace where he ended his first-class career.

GIBBON, SONNY Sonny Gibbon began his career with his hometown club, Merthyr Tydfil, where his father was club chairman. When the Welsh side found themselves in financial difficulties, Sonny was made a professional so that Merthyr could obtain a transfer fee. Gibbon, who had won Welsh Amateur international honours, was signed by Aberdare Athletic, a club that had just lost its Football League status. His performances for Aberdare prompted Merthyr Town to offer him the chance to play League football but after just 25 appearances, Fulham manager Joe Bradshaw paid £700 to bring the full-back to Craven Cottage. Gibbon made his Fulham début in a 4–1 win at Exeter City in March 1929, a match in which Fred Avey scored a hat-trick. Gibbon played in six of the last eleven matches that season, scoring his only goal for the club in a 2–1 win at Swindon Town. An ever-present in 1930–31, he won a Third Division (South) Championship medal the following season. After that, he played mainly for Fulham's reserve side, turning out for the first-team when either Birch or Keeping was injured. He had appeared in 127 League and Cup games when, in April 1935, he was tragically killed in a motor-cycle accident.

GIBBONS, SYD Darlaston-born centre-half Syd Gibbons began his career with his local club Cradley Heath where his performances led to selection for England Juniors against Scotland in 1926. A number of League clubs began to show an interest in him and towards the end of that year he left to join Manchester City. Though he was at Maine Road for four seasons, he made only ten appearances and in July 1930 he came south to play for Fulham. His first game for the Cottagers was in a 3–2 home win over Watford on the opening day of the 1930–31 season after which he was the club's first-choice pivot for eight seasons. Forming an outstanding half-back line with Albert Barrett and Len Oliver, he was ever-present in seasons 1931–32, 1932–33, 1934–35 and 1936–37. During this time he appeared in 114 consecutive League games, helping the club win the Third Division (South) Championship and reach the semi-finals of the FA Cup. He liked nothing more than to join the attack and in November 1934 scored all three goals in a 3–3 draw with Southampton. He had scored 15 goals in 318 League and Cup games when he left Craven Cottage in the summer of 1938 to become player-manager of Worcester City. He later returned to Fulham to work as a scout.

GOALKEEPERS Fulham FC has almost always been extremely well served by its goalkeepers and most of them have been highly popular with the supporters. The club's first outstanding keeper was Jack Fryer who joined Fulham in the summer of 1903 and, in four seasons of Southern League football, appeared in 125 games and won two Championship medals. He had appeared in 170 games for the Cottagers when he retired in 1910. Ernest Beecham was the star of Fulham's FA Cup run of 1925–26 when

Tony Gale

they reached the quarter-finals, after which he won London Combination honours before touring Holland with an England XI. He appeared in 185 games for Fulham. Alf Tootill, known as 'The Birdcatcher', moved to Fulham in the 1932–33 season. He missed very few games over the next five seasons and in 1935–36 he helped the Cottagers to the FA Cup semi-final. He made 214 first-team appearances. Ian Black was signed by Bill Dodgin in the summer of 1950 and in his first season at Craven Cottage was ever-present. Black is one of two Fulham keepers to score a goal, a feat he achieved in the 6–1 defeat at Leicester City in August 1952. He played for Fulham 277 times. In ten years at Craven Cottage, Tony Macedo appeared in 391 League and Cup games, his form winning him ten caps for England at Under-23 level. Peter Mellor was playing non-League football for Witton Albion when Burnley gave him a chance at League level. Despite some impressive performances for the Clarets, the supporters got on his back and in February 1972 he joined Fulham. He was outstanding in the club's run to the FA Cup final in 1975 and missed very few games in his six seasons at Craven Cottage. He had played in 224 games when he fell out with Bobby Campbell and joined Hereford United before later ending his League career with Portsmouth. Gerry Peyton also joined Fulham from Burnley and in ten seasons with the club appeared in 395 League and Cup games. His performances between the posts led to him winning international honours for the Republic of Ireland, 22 of his 33 caps coming whilst he was at Craven Cottage. He left the club in 1986 to join Bournemouth, later playing for Everton before loan spells with a number of clubs. Jim Stannard had two spells with the Cottagers either side of playing for Southend United. During that time he established a club record for the greatest number of first-team appearances for a goalkeeper with 446. He was freed by the Cottagers in the summer of 1995 and joined Gillingham where, in his first season, he kept 29 clean sheets and conceded just 20 goals, a League record.

GOALS The most goals Fulham have scored in any one League game are the 10–1 victory over Ipswich Town on Boxing Day 1963 and the 10–2 defeat of Torquay United on 7 September 1931.

GOALS – CAREER BEST The highest goalscorer in Fulham's history is Gordon Davies who netted 178 goals for the club between 1978–1984 and 1986–1991, 159 in the League, eight in the FA Cup and 11 in the League Cup.

GOALS – INDIVIDUAL Ronnie Rooke holds the club individual scoring record for netting all six of Fulham's goals in their 6–0 third-round FA Cup win over Bury on 7 January 1939. Four Fulham players have scored five goals in a game. The first was Fred Harrison who scored all the club's goals in a 5–1 home win over Stockport County on 5 September 1908. Bedford Jezzard repeated the feat as Fulham beat Hull City 5–0 on 8 October 1955, followed by Jimmy Hill, who netted five of Fulham's goals in a 6–1 win at Doncaster Rovers on 15 March 1958. Steve Earle also achieved the feat on 16 September 1969 when the Cottagers beat Halifax Town 8–0 at the Shay.

GOALS – SEASON The club's highest League goalscorer in any one season is still Frank Newton, who scored 43 League goals in the club's Third Division (South) Championship-winning season of 1931-32. He also scored four goals in that season's FA Cup competition.

GOLDIE, BILLY Left-half Billy Goldie played his early football for Hurlford Thistle before joining Clyde in 1897. A year later he followed his elder brother Archie to Anfield and there in the middle of one spell of 119 consecutive appearances became an ever-present in Liverpool's first Championship-winning side of 1901. He left the Anfield club in January 1904 to join Fulham and made his début in a goalless draw at New Brompton. He won Southern League Championship medals in 1905-06 and 1906-07 before playing against Hull City in the club's inaugural Football League match. He had scored five goals in 179 games for the Cottagers before leaving to play for Leicester Fosse for their First Division début. He stayed for three seasons, appearing in 88 games before leaving to run a pub. An FA disciplinary committee had once felt the need to employ an interpreter in dealing with Goldie during his Liverpool days!

GUEST PLAYERS The 'guest' system was used by all clubs during the two wars. Although at times it was abused almost beyond belief (in that some sides that opposed Fulham had ten or 11 'guests'!) it normally worked sensibly and effectively to the benefit of players, clubs and supporters alike. The most distinguished players to 'guest' for Fulham during the First World War were Harry Hampton (Aston Villa), Danny Shea (Blackburn Rovers), Bill McCracken (Newcastle United) and the Sunderland pair George Holley and Jackie Mordue. In the Second World War, Fulham's 'guest' players included Cliff Bastin (Arsenal), Stan Cullis (Wolves), Ted Drake (Arsenal), Bill Nicholson (Tottenham Hotspur), Billy Wright (Wolverhampton Wanderers), Frank Swift (Manchester City) and Harry Potts (Burnley).

H

HALEY, WILLIAM William Haley began his Football League career with Charlton Athletic but after just one season at the Valley he left to play for Derby County. He struggled to make the first-team at the Baseball Ground, making just 11 appearances in three and a half seasons. Haley was given the chance to resurrect his League career by Fulham manager Joe Bradshaw, joining the Cottagers on a free transfer in the summer of 1928. He made his début in a 2–2 draw at Gillingham on the opening day of the season before scoring on his first appearance at Craven Cottage as Plymouth Argyle were beaten 5–2. Forming a good striking partnership with Jimmy Temple and Fred Avey, Haley ended his first season at the club with 19 goals in 35 games. In 1929–30, Haley was the club's leading scorer with 21 goals in 30 games, a total that included four goals in the 6-1 home win over Watford and hat-tricks against Bristol Rovers (home 6–2), Norwich City (home 3–3) and Merthyr Town (away 4–3). He went on to score 54 goals in 101 games before leaving to join Queen's Park Rangers. After one season at the White City, he left to play non-League football for Dartford and later Sheppey United where he ended his career.

HALOM, VIC Vic Halom was an aggressive and bustling striker who began his Football League career with Charlton Athletic before joining Leyton Orient. After a series of impressive displays, Fulham manager Bobby Robson just beat Brian Clough when he signed the solidly built forward for a fee of £35,000 in November

Vic Halom

1968. After making his Cottagers début in a 2–2 home draw against Portsmouth, Halom struggled with a series of niggling injuries, scoring three goals in just ten appearances. Injuries again hampered his progress in 1969–70 but the following season he made much more of a contribution as Fulham won promtion to the Second Division. He had scored 25 goals in 82 games when in September 1971 he was transferred to Luton Town. After a similar goalscoring record with the Hatters, he moved to Sunderland in February 1973. By the end of that season, Halom had won an FA Cup winners' medal as Sunderland surprisingly beat Leeds United in the 1973 final after scoring one of the goals in the 2–1 semi-final win over Arsenal. In 1973–74, Halom scored 21 goals including a hat-trick in a 3–0 League Cup win over Derby County. He also helped the Wearsiders win promotion as Second Division champions in 1975–76 before leaving to join Oldham Athletic. The popular striker had scored 40 goals in 134 games for Sunderland and his departure was not welcomed by most of the club's supporters. He ended his first season at Boundary Park as the Latic's leading scorer but in February 1980 he moved across the Pennines to end his playing career with Rotherham United. After managing non-League Barrow, he took charge of Rochdale but, failing to find success, returned to non-League circles, first as manager of Burton Albion and then North Shields.

HAMMOND, JIM One of the club's most consistent goalscorers, Jim Hammond was playing as an amateur with Lewes when Fulham signed him in 1928. He made his League début for the Cottagers in a 4–1 defeat at Merthyr Town in March 1929 after which he was a first-team regular for the next nine seasons. In 1929–30, Hammond scored 17 goals including hat-tricks in the wins over Clapton Orient (away 4–2) and Brighton (home 5–1). The following season he was the club's leading scorer with 16 goals, a feat he was to achieve four times, and netted another hat-trick in a 4-2 defeat of Thames. In 1931–32, when Fulham won the Third Division (South) Championship, Hammond netted another hat-trick against Thames (home 8–0) and scored four goals in the 10–2 rout of Torquay United. His 33 goals in 42 games that season earned him a call-up into the England squad and he was 12th man for the match against Austria. In 1934–35, Hammond netted all three goals in the 3–0 win over Plymouth Argyle and scored four in the 7–2 defeat of Sheffield United. The following season he topped the club's scoring charts for the final time, his total of 18 goals including hat-tricks in the wins over Nottingham Forest (home 6–0) and Hull City (home 3–0). Hammond's last hat-trick for the club came in 1937–38 when, after scoring all the club's goals against Coventry City, he ended up on the losing side as the Highfield Road club won 4–3. Hammond's football career ended through injury in 1938 by which time he had scored 150 goals in 342 games. He was also a county cricketer for Sussex and in ten seasons with them scored 4,251 runs at 18.73 and took 428 wickets at 28.71 runs apiece. He later joined the first-class umpires panel.

HARFORD, RAY Ray Harford began his playing career with Charlton Athletic but in two years at The Valley made just three appearances before joining Exeter City. After a further 60 League and Cup appearances for the Grecians, he moved to Lincoln City

Ray Harford

where he remained for four years, playing in 161 games. On leaving Sincil Bank he had brief spells with Mansfield Town and Port Vale before joining Colchester United in 1973. He helped the Layer Road club to win promotion from the Fourth Division but then injury forced his retirement and he became the club's youth team manager. In the summer of 1981, Harford was employed by Fulham manager Malcolm Macdonald as the Cottagers' youth team coach before later stepping up to be first-team coach and assistant manager. When Macdonald left Craven Cottage in April 1984, Harford was given the manager's job for the rest of the season. The Cottagers won five of their remaining six games after which he was appointed on a permanent basis. Sadly, all Harford's efforts at Craven Cottage were undermined by chairman Ernie Clay and in the summer of 1986 he resigned. Moving to First Division Luton Town as assistant to John Moore, Harford became his successor in June 1987 when Moore resigned. He took the Hatters to the League Cup final, where they beat Arsenal 3–2, and to the final of the Simod Cup where they were beaten 4–1 by Reading. Surprisingly, in January 1990 he was sacked and moved to Wimbledon where he was later appointed manager following Bobby Gould's resignation. He too resigned after Keith Curle had been sold to Manchester City without his consent and joined Blackburn Rovers as Kenny Dalglish's assistant. He replaced Dalglish as Blackburn's boss in 1995 but after two years in charge at Ewood Park he was sacked and went to manage West Bromwich Albion before taking over the reins at Queen's Park Rangers.

HARRISON, FRED Fred Harrison began his career with Southampton, developing into one of the best centre-forwards the club has ever produced. It was 1902–03 when he started hitting the headlines for his goalscoring abilities, netting 17 goals in 13 games including five in the wins over Wellingborough Town (home 5–0) and Northampton Town (home 7–0). He helped Southampton win the Southern League Championship that season and again in 1903–04 when he scored 27 goals in 32 games. With his reputation growing all the time, he was the subject of many large offers from big clubs and in 1904 he was given an England trial. Unfortunately in the trial match he was played out of position and failed to gain the international recognition he deserved. Eventually, Harrison, who had scored 83 goals in 153 games, was transferred to Fulham for £1,000, much to the dismay of the Southampton public. He made his Football League début for the Cottagers in November 1907 in a 2–0 defeat at Stockport County before scoring on his home début a week later as Fulham beat Glossop 6–1. Early the following season, Stockport were Fulham's opponents when Harrison scored all five goals in a 5–1 win, ending the season as the club's leading scorer with 13 goals. Unable to find the net for the Cottagers as often as he had for Southampton, Harrison was criticised by a section of the Fulham crowd and in April 1911, after scoring 54 goals in 133 games, he moved to West Ham United with full-back George Redwood. He later played for Bristol City before the First World War, in which he was gassed, ended his playing career.

HAT-TRICKS The club's first hat-trick in the Football League was scored by Robert Dalrymple in the 4–2 win at Lincoln City on 16 October 1907. Ronnie Rooke is one of only two Fulham players to score a hat-trick on his League début, a feat he achieved in the 5–0 home win over West Ham United in November 1936. The other player is Doug McGibbon who netted a hat-trick in the 3–1 win over Plymouth Argyle in January 1947. Harry Hampton of Aston Villa, who 'guested' for Fulham during the First World War, scored a hat-trick on his Cottagers début in an 8–1 win over Southampton on 23 December 1916. Graham Leggatt holds the club record for the fastest hat-trick with three goals in as many minutes in the 10–1 win over Ipswich Town on Boxing Day 1963. Jimmy Hill had gone without a goal for 11 months but in the game against Sheffield Wednesday on Good Friday 1959, he netted a hat-trick in the last quarter of an hour to give Fulham victory by 6–2. When Fulham played Bristol Rovers in the FA Cup fourth-round of 1947–48, director Tommy Trinder offered an overcoat to the first person to score a hat-trick. When Arthur Stevens scored his third goal in the 5–2 win, Trinder was seen hanging over the balcony displaying the coat. The matter was later investigated by the game's authorities who thought an illegal payment might have been made! The greatest number of hat-tricks by a Fulham player in the Football League is eight by Jim Hammond, though he and Ronnie Rooke share the club record with ten in League and Cup games. The last player to score a hat-trick for Fulham was Paul Moody in the 3–0 home win over Preston North End on the final day of the 1998–99 season.

HAYNES, JOHNNY The career of Johnny Haynes was one of the most contradictory in the history of British football. He was the country's first £100-a-week player; he was one of the first to use his fame for advertising and to have an agent; and he was captain of England on 22 occasions. Born and raised in Edmonton,

North London, he should have joined Spurs but after playing for England Schoolboys he chose Fulham. He made his League début for the Cottagers in a 1–1 home draw against Southampton on Boxing Day 1952 and over the next 18 seasons was a first-team regular for the club. When Fulham won promotion to the First Division in 1958–59, Haynes was the club's leading scorer with 26 goals in 34 games including all four goals in the 4–2 home defeat of Lincoln City and hat-tricks in the wins over Sunderland (home 6–2) Leyton Orient (away 5–2) and Rotherham United (home 4–0). In 1961, after former Fulham colleague Jimmy Hill had secured the removal of the £20 maximum wage, club chairman Tommy Trinder declared that 'Johnny is worth £100 a week' and within twenty-four hours the negotiations for a revision of his contract were complete. Haynes gained his major satisfaction from his career with England for whom he won 56 caps. He scored a hat-trick in a 5–0 win over Russia at Wembley in 1958 but his best game in England colours without doubt was the 9–3 defeat of Scotland in 1961. In August 1962, soon after poor displays in the disappointing World Cup in Chile, Haynes was involved in a car crash in Blackpool. It was to end his international career and put his whole playing future in jeopardy. Then aged 29, he did not play for a year and was even told by doctors that he would never play again. The only time it looked at all possible for Haynes and Fulham to part company came after the tragic death of Spurs' Scottish international inside-forward John White in 1964. Bill Nicholson offered £90,000 for his services – it would have been a record fee between British clubs – but the deal did not go through. Johnny Haynes was a perfectionist and a true professional. He did not like to lose and when things went wrong on the field, he had a positive way of expressing his disgust – he stood with his hands on his hips and delivered a withering look! Considering his role as leader of men with Fulham and England, it is strange that Haynes didn't go into management when his playing career ended. He did in fact take over Fulham for 17 days when Bobby Robson was sacked. But he told the Fulham directors that he was not interested and he soon drafted in Bill Dodgin as coach and stood down in favour of him as manager. Haynes scored 157 goals in 657 League and Cup games for the Cottagers and when he left the club in 1970 many expected him to join Jimmy Hill as a television personality but instead he moved to South African football where he won his first honour – as a member of the Durban City side that clinched the League title. Haynes, the King of Craven Cottage, now resides in Edinburgh where he runs a successful dry cleaning business.

Johnny Haynes

HENDERSON, JACKIE Born in Johnshaven in Scotland, Jackie Henderson never played soccer as a schoolboy but joined a youth club side at Kirkintilloch as a teenager. Portsmouth were quick to spot his potential and signed him in January 1949 when they were one of the most successful sides in the country. He soon established himself as a first-team regular at Fratton Park and won the first of seven Scottish caps against Sweden in May 1953. After 233 League and Cup appearances for Pompey in which he scored 73 goals, he moved to Wolverhampton Wanderers in March 1958 but only stayed eight months before he was on the move again. When he signed for Arsenal, the Scot recaptured some of his old form, playing on the wing as he had done for most of his time at Portsmouth. In January 1962 he left Highbury and joined Fulham, making his début for the Cottagers in a 4–3 home defeat at the hands of Chelsea. He went on to score nine goals in 56 games for Fulham but was sadly past his best. His last move took him to Poole Town in the summer of 1964.

HILL, JIMMY Jimmy Hill's enthusiasm for the game of football has led to him being a player, union leader, manager, director, television personality and even an emergency linesman! Hill was first spotted by Reading manager Ted Drake playing for his regiment whilst on National Service and turned out as an amateur for the then Elm Park club. After not being offered terms he moved to Brentford before joining Fulham in March 1952. He scored in his first game for the Cottagers but they went down 4–2 at Blackpool. Hill was a first-team regular at Craven Cottage for the next nine seasons, helping the side win promotion to the First Division in 1958–59. The previous season, Hill had scored five goals in a 6–1 win at Doncaster Rovers and netted six goals in the club's run to the FA Cup semi-finals. During the club's promotion-winning season of 1958–59, Hill's total of 16 goals included a hat-trick in a 6–2 defeat of Sheffield Wednesday. He went on to score 52 goals in 297 games before a knee injury brought his career to a close in 1961. In 1956, Hill had become chairman of the Professional Footballers' Association and shot to prominence when he fought to rid the game of the restrictive £20-a-week maximum wage. In November 1961, Jimmy Hill joined Coventry City as manager and in 1963–64 led the club to the Third Division Championship. The Second Division title followed three years later but in September 1968, Hill left Highfield Road after receiving a lucrative offer to become head of sport with London Weekend Television. A qualified FA coach and referee, he once made an appearance as an emergency linesman at Arsenal when the original official was injured. Hill was working for television that day at Highbury and when a call was made for a replacement, he took up the challenge. In October 1972 he left London Weekend Television to set up his own television consultancy group and became commercial manager at Fulham. He returned to Coventry as managing director in April 1975 and later as chairman before leaving to become a director of Charlton Athletic in the summer of 1983. He left Charlton in 1987 to become chairman of Fulham, a position he held until 1997.

HINDSON, JAMES On leaving school, James Hindson joined Hylton Colliery as a miner and played full-back for their football team in the Wearside League. His impressive performances led to Sunderland securing his services but after failing to make the grade, he returned to non-League football with Spennymoor United. He later had a brief spell as an amateur with Middlesbrough before Fulham manager Ned Liddell offered him professional terms in the summer of 1930. He had to wait until January 1932 before making his League début in a 2–0 home defeat by Gillingham but after six appearances he gave way to Arthur Tilford. After being in and out of the side the following season, he started the 1933–34 campaign as the club's first-choice right-back but in only the fourth game he broke his leg in a 4–3 defeat at Blackpool. He recovered to take his total of League and Cup appearances to 113 before retiring and joining the Craven Cottage training staff.

HINTON, TED Northern Ireland international goalkeeper Ted Hinton began his career with Glentoran, appearing for them in the 1942 Irish Cup final defeat by Linfield, before leaving to join Distillery. Just before the resumption of League football in 1946–47, Fulham manager Jack Peart persuaded Hinton to cross the Irish Sea and he made his début for the Cottagers in a 3–2 defeat at West Ham United. Despite not keeping a clean sheet in his first 12 games for Fulham, Hinton won the first of his seven full caps when he was chosen to play against Scotland at Hampden Park. The result was a goalless draw and Hinton had an outstanding game! Though he only missed one game in 1947–48, Hinton lost his place to Doug Flack early the following season and in the summer of 1949 joined Millwall for £1,500. He made 91 League appearances for the Lions before returning to Ireland to play for Ballymena and later Bangor.

HOGAN, JIMMY Jimmy Hogan was an average player who won two Southern League Championship medals and appeared in an FA Cup semi-final with Fulham before going to coach in Holland. Two years later, he went to Austria where he formed a famous partnership with Hugo Meisl. These two were given much of the credit for the development of the game in Europe. In 1934, Hogan returned to England to manage Fulham but the players and directors did not like his training methods and tactics and he was relieved of his duties whilst in hospital recovering from illness. After a short spell in Austria again, where he helped the national side to the 1936 Olympic football final, he returned to these shores to take charge of Aston Villa in November 1936. He led Villa to promotion from the Second Division and to an FA Cup semi-final but the Second World War ended his connection with the club, although Villa were one of three clubs to benefit from his development of the youth scheme. Later he went to coach in Hungary and inspired the great Puskas–Hidegkuti Hungarian side that beat England 6–3 at Wembley in 1953.

HOME MATCHES Fulham's biggest win in the Football League is the 10–1 defeat of Ipswich Town on 26 December 1963. The Cottagers also beat Torquay United 10–2 on 7 September 1931. The club have also scored eight goals in home matches on two occasions, beating Thames Association 8–0 on 28 March 1932 and Swansea Town 8–1 on 22 January 1938. The club's worst home defeat is 6–1 by Bradford on 21 February 1914 whilst they have also been beaten 6–3 by Aston Villa in 1965–66 and 6–4 by Leicester City in 1952–53.

HOME SEASONS Fulham have never gone through a complete Football League season with an undefeated home record but have lost just one match on three occasions – 1912–13, 1948–49 and 1998-99. In this latter season the Cottagers won 19 of their home matches, a club record.

HONOURS The major honours achieved by the club are:

Division Two Champions 1948–49 1998–99
Division Two Runners-Up 1958–59
Division Three (South) Champions 1931–32
Division Three Runners-Up 1970–71 1996–97
FA Cup Runners-Up 1974–75
Anglo-Scottish Cup Runners-Up 1975

HOPKINS, JEFF Welsh international Jeff Hopkins was still an apprentice when he made his Fulham début in a 4–2 defeat at Huddersfield Town on the final day of the 1980–81 season. The following season he appeared in 35 games, helping the club win promotion from the Third Division. Hopkins, who initially played at right-back, moved to centre-half following the

Jeff Hopkins

departure of Roger Brown to Bournemouth and though he struggled in the air against some of the bigger opposition forwards, he went on to be a fine central defender. He had scored six goals in 257 League and Cup games when, in the summer of

1988, Crystal Palace paid £240,000 for his services. He played in 93 games for the Eagles before, following a loan spell with Plymouth Argyle, he joined Bristol Rovers on a free transfer. His stay at Twerton Park was brief and in July 1992 he moved to Reading where this dedicated professional not only captained the side but helped out with the coaching of the younger players before injury forced him to quit the first-class game after 123 appearances for the Royals.

HORSFIELD, GEOFF Geoff Horsfield began his Football League career with Scarborough but after failing to make much headway went into non-League football, first with Halifax Town and then with Witton Albion before rejoining the Shaymen in May 1997. In his first season back at the Shay he helped Halifax win the Conference Championship and election to the Football League. After making a good start to the 1998–99 season with the Yorkshire club, having scored eight goals in 14 games, Fulham boss Kevin Keegan paid £325,000 for his services in October 1998. He made his début as a substitute for Paul Peschisolido, scoring the Cottagers' last goal in a 4–1 win over Walsall. Holding the ball up well, Horsfield became a great favourite with the Fulham crowd as the Cottagers went on to win the Second Division Championship. Topping the club's scoring charts with 17 League and Cup goals, his performances were recognised by his peers with selection to the PFA award-winning side.

HOUGHTON, RAY An industrious midfield player, Ray Houghton began his League career with West Ham United, making his début as a substitute at Arsenal in May 1982. That was the only chance he got at Upton Park and, released by John Lyall, he joined Fulham. He made his début for the Cottagers in a 1–1 home draw against Rotherham United on the opening day of the 1982–83 season, going on to be one of six ever-presents as the club finished fourth in Division Two. After missing only two games the following season, Houghton was ever-present again in 1984–85. He had scored 21 goals in 145 games for Fulham when in September 1985 he was transferred to Oxford United for a fee of £125,000. Newly promoted to the First Division, the Manor Ground club went on to win the League Cup, Houghton scoring the second goal in a 3–0 win over Queen's Park Rangers. Also in his first season with Oxford, Houghton won the first of 73 caps for the Republic of Ireland. Signed by Liverpool in October 1987, he went on to win a League Championship medal in his first season. The following term he played in every game, picking up an FA Cup winners' medal. During the summer of 1992 he joined Aston Villa for a fee of £900,000. He made 115 League and Cup appearances for Villa before lending his experience to Crystal Palace, signing for the Eagles in March 1995 for £300,000. Two years later he joined Reading on a free transfer, but left the club at the end of the 1998–99 season.

HUNDRED GOALS Fulham have scored more than 100 League goals in a season on one occasion, in 1931–32, when the club scored 111 goals from 42 matches to win the Third Division (South) Championship. The leading goalscorer was Frank 'Bonzo' Newton with 43, whilst his striking partner Jim Hammond netted 31.

I

ICETON, JAKE Goalkeeper Jake Iceton was working down the pit and playing for his local club West Auckland when Hull City offered him terms. Unable to make the grade with the Boothferry Park club, he was released and returned to non-League football with Shildon. His performances for the north-east club led to Fulham manager Ned Liddell offering him another chance of League football and in August 1930, at the age of 26, he made his Football League début in a 3–2 home win over Watford. Iceton was the club's first-choice keeper for the next two seasons, winning a Third Division (South) Championship medal in 1931–32, when he kept 12 clean sheets in 33 games. After losing his place to Alf Tootill, Iceton, who had made 99 League and Cup appearances for the Cottagers, was given a free transfer to Aldershot. However, he found it difficult to hold down a regular first-team spot at the Recreation Ground and moved to Clapton Orient where he played until retiring on the outbreak of the Second World War.

INTERNATIONAL MATCHES Craven Cottage has played host to one full international match, when England met Wales on 18 March 1907. The game ended all-square at 1–1 with Sheffield Wednesday's Jimmy Stewart scoring for England.

INTERNATIONAL PLAYERS Fulham's most capped player (that is caps gained while players were registered with the club) is Johnny Haynes, who won 56 caps for England. The following is a complete list of players who have gained full international honours for England, Scotland, Wales, Northern Ireland and the Republic of Ireland.

England	*Caps*
Johnny Arnold	1
Albert Barrett	1
George Cohen	37
Johnny Haynes	56
Bedford Jezzard	2
Jim Langley	3
Len Oliver	1
Frank Osborne	2
Jim Taylor	2

Northern Ireland	*Caps*
George Best	5
Bobby Brennan	1
Johnny Campbell	2
Joe Connor*	1
Ted Hinton	5
Hugh Kelly	2
Jack McClelland	1
Alex Steele	2
Maik Taylor	4

Scotland	*Caps*
Graham Leggatt	11
Jimmy Sharp	1

Wales	*Caps*
Chris Coleman	8
Gordon Davies	14
Jeff Hopkins	14
Cliff Jones	2

Republic of Ireland	*Caps*
Jimmy Conway	18
John Dempsey	7
Jimmy Dunne	1
Robin Lawler	8
Turlough O'Connor	1
Sean O'Driscoll	3
Gerry Peyton	22

Billy Richards	1
Kit Symons	4
Sid Thomas	4

* The first Fulham player to be capped, against England on 12 March 1904 in Belfast.

J

JEZZARD, BEDFORD One of the Cottagers' best-ever centre-forwards, who later became one of the club's most successful managers, Bedford Jezzard was working on the staff of the Old Merchant Taylor's sports ground when Fulham asked him to join them in the summer of 1948. He made his first-team début in a 2–1 defeat at Cardiff City but held his place in the side for the remainder of that 1948–49 season, scoring six goals in 30 games, as the club won the Second Division Championship. Over the next three seasons, Jezzard was a regular in the club's First Division side but it was following the club's relegation to the Second Division that he developed into a prolific goalscorer. An ever-present in 1952–53, he was the club's top-scorer with 35 goals, a total which included his first hat-trick in a 4–1 home win over Rotherham United. The following season, he was again ever-present and netted 38 goals including four in a 5–2 defeat of Derby County and a hat-trick against Plymouth Argyle (home 3–1). It was during this season that Jezzard established a club record when he found the net in nine consecutive League games. In 1954–55, Jezzard scored in each of the club's first seven League games, ending the season as joint top scorer with Bobby Robson. In 1955–56, Jezzard, who revelled in heavy conditions, scored four goals in the 5–1 defeat of Burnley and then went one better later in the season, netting all five goals in the 5–0 rout of Hull City. An England international, he was on tour with an FA XI in South Africa when he received an ankle injury which ended his career prematurely at the age of 28. Jezzard, who had scored

154 goals in 306 League and Cup games, became the club's youth team coach before being appointed the Cottagers' manager in June 1958. In his first season in charge, he led the club to promotion to the First Division as runners-up. The rest of Jezzard's time in charge was all spent in the top-flight, but following the sale of Alan Mullery to Spurs in March 1964, a transfer arranged without his knowledge, he left the club to run a pub in Stamford Brook near Hammersmith.

JUBILEE FUND The League Benevolent Fund was launched in 1938, fifty years after the start of the Football League, to help players who had fallen on hard times. It was decided that the best way to raise funds was for sides to play local derby games without taking into account League status. Just before the start of the 1938–39 season, the Cottagers drew 3–3 with West Ham United at Upton Park, an own goal by Mike Keeping allowing the Hammers to draw level in the closing minutes. When the two sides met in a Second Division match two weeks later, Fulham won 3–2.

K

KEEGAN, KEVIN The current England manager Kevin Keegan began his Football League career with Scunthorpe United, for whom he had made 124 appearances when Bill Shankly plucked him from the obscurity of the lower divisions in 1971 for a fee of £35,000. He hit Anfield like a tornado. Converted from a deep-lying winger to striker, he made his Liverpool début against Nottingham Forest in the opening match of the 1971–72 season and scored after seven minutes. His all-action approach won over the fans and he soon became the idol of the Kop. Keegan was brave, quick and completely inexhaustible. His understanding up front with John Toshack appeared to border on telepathy. Selected for England in November 1972, he won his first three caps, out of a total 63, against Wales. In his six years at Anfield, he won three League Championship medals, two UEFA Cup winner's medals, an FA Cup winners' medal (1974) when Liverpool beat Newcastle United, and a European Cup winners' medal in 1977 against Borussia Moenchengladbach. This was Keegan's last game for Liverpool. He left Anfield to join SV Hamburg for £500,000, a fee which made him England's most expensive and best-paid player. At Hamburg, Keegan was twice European Footballer of the Year but in February 1980 Southampton manager Lawrie McMenemy swooped to sign him. In 1980–81, Keegan topped the First Division scoring charts with 26 goals, to win the Shoot-Adidas Golden Boot award. After joining Newcastle United in August 1982, he led the Magpies back into the First Division before deciding to retire from playing. Keegan was a folk hero on

Kevin Keegan

Tyneside and he was welcomed back with open arms when he was appointed manager of the club in February 1992. In 1992–93, United won the First Division Championship, eight points clear of runners-up West Ham United. During his time at St James Park, the Magpies never finished out of the top six in the Premier League and were runners-up on two occasions. However, in January 1997 he caused consternation on Tyneside with his sudden, sensational resignation as Newcastle manager. In September 1997 Keegan was appointed chief operating officer of Fulham, with Ray Wilkins as team manager. Despite a run of poor results, the Cottagers still made that season's play-offs but Wilkins lost his job. Keegan took over team affairs but the change failed to halt the slide and Grimsby put paid to the club's hopes of survival in the play-offs. The following season, with Fulham leading the Second Division, Keegan became England's caretaker manager, adamant that he would not abandon his duties at Craven Cottage. However, after taking Fulham to the Second Division Championship, Keegan, who received a mixed reception on the final day of the season, decided to take the England job full-time.

KEEPING, MIKE Full-back Mike Keeping began his Football League career with Southampton, whom he joined from Milford-on-Sea in December 1920. Keeping developed into a 'classic' left-back, being particularly skilful with his left foot and very fast. He became Saints' captain and in 1926 toured Canada with the FA. In 1931 he represented the Football League and was expected to play for England that year but appendicitis ruled him out for the rest of the 1931–32 season. Keeping had scored ten goals in 265 games for Southampton when, in February 1933, he was allowed to join Fulham along with Johnny Arnold for a fee of £5,100. He made his Fulham début in a 3–3 home draw against Bury and played in the remaining 14 games of the season as the club pushed hard for promotion to the top-flight. Sadly, the Cottagers had to settle for third place in Division Two. Keeping was a regular member of the Fulham side for the seven seasons leading up to the outbreak of the Second World War, scoring seven goals in 217 League and Cup games. After the war, Keeping coached Real Madrid, later managing sides in Denmark, Holland, France and North Africa. In 1959 he returned to manage Southern League Poole Town.

KEETCH, BOBBY An uncompromising and tough-tackling centre-half, Bobby Keetch began his career with West Ham United but, unable to make the grade, he joined Fulham in April 1959. He had to wait until September 1961 before making his first-team début, in a League Cup tie against Sheffield United (home 1–1), and April 1962 before playing in his first League game against Leyton Orient (home 0–2). Keetch went on to score two goals in 120 games, all before manager Vic Buckingham gave him a free transfer. Keetch, who loved Fulham, was devastated and decided to retire. However, Queen's Park

Rangers persuaded him to return to the game, and on doing so, he appeared in 56 games as the Loftus Road club rose from the Third to the First Division. Keetch left Queen's Park Rangers in 1969 to play for Durban City but nowadays he travels the world as an importer.

KELLY, HUGH Hugh Kelly's early days in sport were spent playing handball and Gaelic football in his native Ireland. In 1939 he signed for Irish League club Glenavon as an inside-left but during the Second World War he was converted to goalkeeper whilst playing for Belfast Celtic. In March 1949 he joined Fulham but had to wait six months before making his début in a 1–1 home draw against Chelsea. In November 1949, Kelly won the first of four international caps for Northern Ireland but let in nine goals as England triumphed 9–2 at Maine Road. Kelly had made just 27 appearances for Fulham when he joined Southampton in exchange for Ian Black in the summer of 1950. Unable to win a regular place at The Dell, he joined Exeter City where he ended his League career after three seasons with the Grecians. He later played non-League football for Weymouth.

KELSO, PHIL Phil Kelso was manager of Hibernian before taking charge of Woolwich Arsenal in 1904. At Plumstead, he took the club to two FA Cup semi-finals but after four years in charge, returned to Scotland to run a hotel at Largs in the Firth of Clyde. However, twelve months later, the Fulham board managed to persuade him to replace Harry Bradshaw who had left to become secretary of the Southern League. The abrasive Scot was insistent that anyone who played for Fulham should not only neither drink nor smoke, but should also live in London. Kelso was in charge at Craven Cottage for fifteen years, during which time he brought a number of famous internationals to the club. Though they failed to win promotion to the First Division, Kelso helped steer the club through the difficult years of the First World War. After the Armistice, Kelso began to build up a fine side but, following the Barney Travers bribery scandal, he lost a lot of credibility and in 1924 ended his involvement with the game.

KEY, JOHNNY Winger Johnny Key joined Fulham straight from school and, after working his way up through the ranks, made his first-team début in a 4–0 FA Cup win over Yeovil Town in January 1958. His League début came nine months later as Fulham went down 1–0 at home to Liverpool. Over the next seven seasons, Key was an important member of the Fulham side, many of his 37 goals in 181 games resulting from spectacular strikes outside the penalty area. At the end of the 1965–66 season, Key was one of a number of players allowed to leave Craven Cottage by Fulham manager Vic Buckingham. He joined Coventry City, who were managed by former Cottager, Jimmy Hill. In his first season at Highfield Road, Key helped the Sky Blues to win the Second Division Championship but, towards the end of the club's first season in the top-flight, Key, who had scored seven goals in 28 League games, moved to join Orient where he ended his first-class career.

L

LACY, JOHN Liverpool-born John Lacy played non-League football for Marine but then gave up any thoughts of becoming a professional footballer to pursue a Bachelor of Science Degree at the London School of Economics. Whilst studying, he played for London University, who were coached by former England and Fulham full-back, George Cohen. After Lacy had gained his degree, Cohen persuaded him to join the amateur staff at Craven Cottage. He made his League début as a substitute for John Cutbush in a 3–1 defeat at Cardiff City in November 1972 after which he developed rapidly, helped by the vast experience of Bobby Moore and Alan Mullery. Lacy played for the Cottagers in the 1975 FA Cup final defeat against West Ham United. Attracting the attention of the bigger clubs, Lacy, who had scored eight goals in 192 games, left Craven Cottage in the summer of 1978 to join Tottenham Hotspur for £200,000. A regular at the heart of the Spurs defence for most of his first season with the White Hart Lane club, his place came under increasing threat with the emergence of Paul Miller. Though he stayed at Spurs until July 1983, taking his total appearances to 174, his opportunities were now few and far between and it came as no surprise when he joined Crystal Palace. After a spell in Norway, he spent a year with Barnet and three more at St Albans before joining Wivenhoe.

LAMPE, DEREK England Youth international Derek Lampe joined Fulham in the summer of 1952 after impressing in a trial. He

John Lacy

worked his way up through the ranks and made his League début in a 4–1 home defeat by West Ham United on the opening day of the 1956–57 season. Though Fulham's defence conceded 14 goals in the opening four fixtures of that campaign, Lampe kept his place, missing just two games as the Cottagers rallied to end the season in 11th place in Division Two. In fact, Lampe's performances in the heart of the Fulham defence earned him selection for the England Under-20 side whom he captained to a 2–1 win over Hungary at White Hart Lane. Though Lampe remained at Craven Cottage until 1964, he only appeared in a total of 96 League and Cup games as his career was ruined by injury.

Jim Langley

LANGLEY, JIM Full-back Jim Langley was born in Kilburn in 1929 and, after playing as an amateur for Yiewsley, Hayes and Brentford, he had nine League games as an outside-left for Leeds United. On moving to Brighton and Hove Albion he was converted into a full-back, going on to make 174 appearances for the Seagulls. His performances for the Goldstone Ground club led to his winning three England 'B' caps and representing the Football League. He was transferred to Fulham in February 1957, making his League début for the Cottagers in a 3–1 home defeat at the hands of Bury. Langley, a great favourite of the Craven Cottage faithful, was a first-team regular for Fulham for eight seasons. During that time he won three full caps for England, the first against Scotland in 1958, and helped the club reach two FA Cup semi-finals and win promotion to the First Division in 1958–59. He had scored 33 goals in 356 League and Cup games for Fulham when in July 1965 he was surprisingly sold to Queen's Park Rangers for £5,000. Ever-present in his first season with the Loftus Road club, he was a key member of the 1966–67 side which won the League Cup and the Third Division Championship. Shortly afterwards, Langley, who was only the second full-back in the League to score over fifty League goals, left to manage non-League Hillingdon Borough, whom he took to Wembley in 1971. After a spell as coach at Crystal Palace, the popular Langley now lives in West Drayton where he is steward of the local British Legion club.

LARGEST CROWD On 8 October 1938 at Craven Cottage a record crowd of 49,335 saw the Cottagers beat Milwall 2–1 in a Second Division game with goals from Woodward and Evans.

LATE FINISHES During the Second World War, in both 1939–40 and 1940–41, the season continued into June. On 6 June 1940, Fulham lost 2–1 at home to Southampton whilst on 9 June 1941 they lost by a similar score at Tottenham Hotspur. Fulham's final match of the season against Millwall at The Den on 14 June 1947 is the latest date for the finish of any Cottagers' season.

LAWLER, ROBIN Republic of Ireland international Robin Lawler played his early football for Home Park before joining Distillery. Two seasons later he was on the move again, this time to Drumcondra before signing for Belfast Celtic. It was from here that Fulham signed Lawler in the summer of 1945 but he had to wait until December 1949 before making his first-team début in a 2–1 defeat at Charlton Athletic. In fact, Lawler made just 11 League appearances over the next three seasons and it was 1952–53 before he established himself as a regular in the Cottagers side. Towards the end of that season he won the first of eight caps for the Republic of Ireland when he played against Austria, thus becoming the first Fulham player to represent the Republic. Lawler, who was noted for his long throw-ins, went on to appear in 299 games for the Cottagers, helping them to win promotion to the First Division in 1958–59. On leaving Craven Cottage, he went to play non-League football for Yiewsley but a series of injuries forced him to retire.

LEADING GOALSCORERS The only Fulham player to have ended a season as the Football League's leading divisional goalscorer is Gordon Davies who, in 1981–82, headed the Third Division scoring charts with 24 goals.

LEAGUE GOALS – CAREER HIGHEST Gordon Davies holds the Craven Cottage record for the most League goals with a career total of 159 goals in his two spells with the club, 1978–1984 and 1986–1991.

LEAGUE GOALS – LEAST CONCEDED During the 1922–23 season, the Cottagers conceded just 32 goals to finish tenth in Division Two, and again in 1998–99 in winning the Second Division Championship.

LEAGUE GOALS – MOST INDIVIDUAL Frank Newton holds the Fulham record for the most League goals scored in a season with 43 in the Third Division (South) Championship-winning season of 1931–32.

LEAGUE GOALS – MOST SCORED Fulham's highest goals tally in the Football League – 111 – came in the Third Division (South) Championship-winning season of 1931–2.

LEAGUE VICTORY – HIGHEST On Boxing Day 1963 Fulham beat Ipswich Town 10–1 at Craven Cottage. Graham Leggatt scored four goals and Bobby Howfield a hat-trick, whilst the Cottagers' other scorers were Alan Mullery, Bobby Robson and Maurice Cook. The club's previous highest League victory had been the 10–2 victory over Torquay United in a Third Division (South) match on 7 September 1931.

LEGGATT, GRAHAM Scottish international Graham Leggatt began his career with Aberdeen, winning Scottish League Cup and Scottish Cup medals before joining Fulham for £15,000 in the summer of 1958. With the Dons, Leggatt had scored 90 goals in 140 games including the winning goal against St Mirren in the 1955 League Cup final. Leggatt scored on his Fulham début as the Cottagers beat Stoke City 6–1 on the opening day of the

1958–59 season. He ended the campaign with 21 goals in 36 games including a hat-trick in a 3–2 win at Middlesbrough as the club won promotion to the First Division. In the club's first season in the top-flight, Leggatt was the leading scorer, his total of 18 goals in 28 games including four in the 5–0 defeat of Leeds United and all three in the 3–3 draw at Manchester United. Leggatt topped the club's scoring charts again in 1960–61 with the best return of his Fulham career, 23 goals in 36 games including hat-tricks in the wins over Bolton Wanderers (away 3–0) and Leicester City (home 4–2). When Fulham beat Ipswich Town 10–1 on Boxing Day 1963, Leggatt netted a three-minute hat-trick, a First Division record. He topped the scoring charts again that season and in 1965–66 when his total of 15 goals included a hat-trick in a 6–3 defeat at home to Aston Villa. The last of Leggatt's eight hat-tricks, a post-war record, came in the 4–2 home win over Leicester City in December 1966. Surprisingly, Vic Buckingham sold Leggatt, who had scored 134 goals in 280 games, to Birmingham City for £15,000. By now he had lost most of his speed and looked out of condition and, in summer1968, he joined Rotherham United, where he ended his League career. After spells as Aston Villa's assistant coach and player with Bromsgrove Rovers, he emigrated to Canada where, after managing Toronto Star, he now hosts his own soccer show for a Toronto-based television station.

LEWINGTON, RAY After working his way through the ranks at Chelsea, where he captained the junior and reserve sides, he made his League début for the Stamford Bridge club in February 1976. Next season, he helped the Blues win promotion to the First Division but, after the appointment of Danny Blanchflower, Lewington, who had made 92 appearances for Chelsea, was allowed to try his luck in Canada with Vancouver Whitecaps. On his return to these shores, he made 30 appearances for Wimbledon before joining Fulham in March 1980. He made his début in a 3–2 win at West Ham United, going on to be a first-team regular for the next six seasons. He helped the club win promotion to the Second Division in 1981–82, occasionally captaining the team. He left Craven Cottage in the summer of 1985 to play for Sheffield United but after just one season and 41 appearances for the Bramhall Lane club, he rejoined the Cottagers. Appointed the club's first player-manager, he remained in charge until June 1990 when, having scored 24 goals in 269 games, he became the club's chief coach. Ray Lewington is now on the coaching staff of Crystal Palace.

Ray Lewington

LEYLAND DAF CUP The Leyland Daf Cup replaced the Sherpa Van Trophy for the 1989–90 season. Fulham lost both of their preliminary round games at Peterborough United and at home to Notts County by 1–0. In 1990–91 the Cottagers qualified for the knockout stages of the competition after winning 2–0 at Leyton Orient and drawing 1–1 at home to Brentford. However, in the first-round, they went down 2–1 at Mansfield Town to end their interest in the competition.

LIDDELL, NED As a player, Ned Liddell graduated through local Wearside Leagues before signing for Sunderland. He never made Sunderland's first-team and in 1905 moved to Southampton. After just one appearance he moved to Gainsborough Trinity, and then to Clapton Orient for whom he made 201 appearances.

He subsequently played for Southend and Arsenal before working in the shipyards during the First World War. After the hostilities, he entered management with Southend before taking over the reins at Queen's Park Rangers where he became the club's first Football League manager. In 1925 he joined Fulham as a scout but, following the departure of Joe Bradshaw four years later, Liddell was invited to manage the Cottagers. During the two seasons he was in charge, his teams played open attacking football but failed to make a serious challenge for promotion. His relationship with the club chairman John Dean was not an easy one and in 1931, Liddell, who was asked to stay on as scout, was replaced by James McIntyre. Not surprisingly he felt he couldn't continue to work at Craven Cottage and after acting as a scout for West Ham United he managed Luton Town. He later worked as a scout for Chelsea, Portsmouth, Brentford and Spurs.

LIPSHAM, HERBERT Speedy winger Herbert Lipsham began his career with his home-town club Chester before joining Crewe Alexandra in 1898. After two seasons with the Gresty Road club he left to play First Division football for Sheffield United. He appeared in two FA Cup finals for the Blades, picking up a winners' medal in 1902 when United beat Southampton 2–1. Whilst with the Yorkshire club, Lipsham won full international honours for England when he played against Wales at Wrexham in 1902. He had scored 34 goals in 259 games for the Blades, when in April 1908, Fulham manager Harry Bradshaw brought him to Craven Cottage. He made his Fulham début in a 5–1 win over Leicester Fosse, creating three of the goals. He was the club's first choice outside-left in 1908–9 but midway through the following season he lost his place to Willie Walker and after scoring five goals in 59 games, left to become manager of Millwall. He later emigrated to Canada where he met with tragedy. After losing a hand in a timber-yard accident, he died in a train crash at the age of 54.

LIVINGSTONE, DUGGIE Duggie Livingstone joined Glasgow Celtic as a youngster but being unable to break into the side on a regular basis, he moved south to join Everton. A cool, calculating defender, his lack of speed let him down and, after appearing in exactly 100 League and Cup games, he moved to Plymouth Argyle. In and out of the side at Home Park, he returned to Scotland to play for Aberdeen but two seasons later he returned to the Liverpool area to play for Tranmere Rovers. He was later appointed trainer at Exeter City before moving to

Sheffield United in a similar capacity. In 1949 he became manager of Sparta Rotterdam but within a couple of years he was on the move again, this time to become the Republic of Ireland team manager. He later managed Belgium and took them to the 1954 World Cup finals before being appointed manager of Newcastle United. In his first season at St James Park, the Magpies won the FA Cup but, after a furious row with the Newcastle board, he left to take charge at Fulham. Though he stayed at Craven Cottage for only two years, this most underrated of managers laid the foundations for the club's success at the end of the 1950s and early 1960s. In 1957–58 he led the club to the FA Cup semi-finals and fifth place in Division Two and the board were keen to offer him a new contract but his wife couldn't settle in the south and he left to end his managerial career with Chesterfield.

LLOYD, BARRY Barry Lloyd began his League career with Chelsea, making his début for the Stamford Bridge club against West Bromwich Albion in April 1967. Over the next three seasons, the England Youth international made just 14 appearances for the Blues and in February 1969 decided to drop down a division and join Fulham in order to play regular first-team football. Lloyd joined the Cottagers in exchange for John Dempsey plus £35,000 and made his début in a 2–0 home defeat at the hands of Carlisle United. Fulham were relegated at the end of that season, but within two years under Lloyd's captaincy they had won promotion to the Second Division. Midfielder Lloyd, who was a great club man, helped Fulham reach the FA Cup final in 1975 but was on the substitutes' bench as the Cottagers lost 2–0 to West Ham United. Lloyd had scored 30 goals in 289 League and Cup games when he left Craven Cottage in October 1976 to join Hereford United. After just one season at Edgar Street he moved to Brentford when his former manager Bill Dodgin took over the reins in 1977. His one season with the Griffin Park club was a huge success as the Bees won promotion to the Third Division. After a spell as manager of Yeovil Town he took charge of Worthing, helping them from the Isthmian League Second Division to runners-up in the Premier Division in seasons 1983–84 and 1984–85. In 1986 he joined Brighton and Hove Albion as assistant manager to Alan Mullery, replacing the former England international on his departure. The Seagulls were relegated in 1986–87, but Lloyd took them straight back as runners-up and, despite the club's huge debts and the crowd calling for him to be sacked, the board continued to give him their backing until 1994 when he lost his job. He is now back at Worthing as a consultant.

Barry Lloyd

LOCK, KEVIN An England Youth international, Kevin Lock had the unenviable task of filling Bobby Moore's number six shirt at West Ham United. In 1973 Lock won three England Under-23 caps and two years later won an FA Cup winners' medal when the Hammers beat Fulham in the final. He went on to play in 161 League and Cup games before joining Fulham in May 1978 for a fee of £60,000. Lock made his Cottagers début in a 3–1 defeat at Bristol Rovers on the opening day of the 1978–79 campaign, going on to be a regular in the Fulham side for the next seven seasons. He helped them win promotion from the Third Division in 1981–82 and the following season was instrumental in the club almost reaching the top-flight. Lock, who was the club's regular penalty-taker, scored 29 goals in 237 League and Cup games before linking up with Bobby Moore again at Southend United.

LOWE, EDDIE Eddie Lowe began his Football League career with Aston Villa, joining the Midlands club in the summer of 1945. In the first four seasons following the resumption of League football after the Second World War, Lowe played in 117 games for the Villa Park club, his performances winning him full international honours for England. He won three full caps, one of them in a 10–0 rout of Portugal. In May 1950, he and his brother Reg joined Fulham in a combined £15,000 deal. Able to play at full-back or wing-half, he made his début for the Cottagers in a 1–0 defeat at Manchester United on the opening day of the 1950–51 season. After that, Lowe missed very few games over the next thirteen seasons and was ever-present in 1956–57. After helping the club win promotion to the First Division in 1958–59 he pitted his wits against the best inside-forwards in the top-flight and often came out on top. Unlucky not to add to his total of international caps whilst with the Cottagers, he had scored ten goals in 511 League and Cup games when he decided to hang up his boots at the end of the 1962–63 season. Lowe went into management with Notts County but had a disastrous first season in charge as the Magpies were relegated from the bottom of the Third Division. In an effort to rectify matters, he made a comeback as a player just before his 40th birthday and made nine appearances but County finished in mid-table in 1964–65 and he was sacked. He later worked as a purchasing manager for a central heating company in Nottingham, whilst scouting for Plymouth Argyle.

LOWEST The lowest number of goals scored by Fulham in a single Football League season was 39 in 1973–74 when the club finished 13th in the Second Division. The club's lowest points record in the Football League occurred in 1968–69 when the Cottagers gained just 25 points and finished bottom of the Second Division.

M

McCLELLAND, JACK Northern Ireland international goalkeeper Jack McClelland began his career with Gillingham before joining Arsenal in October 1960. Though initially he was unable to wrest the regular goalkeeping position from Jack Kelsey, he grabbed his chance when the Welsh international keeper's career ended during the 1962 World Cup. However, after playing in 49 first-team games he suffered a serious injury and was out of the side for four months. Unable to oust Jim Furnell, he left to join Fulham, playing his first game for the Cottagers in a 3–2 defeat at Stoke City in December 1965, a year after joining the club. Over the next four seasons he shared the goalkeeping duties with Tony Macedo but, after 57 appearances and a loan spell at Lincoln City, he left to play non-League football for Barnet. It was around this time that his health deteriorated and in March 1976 he died at the age of just thirty-five.

McDONALD, JACK Jack McDonald joined Wolves just before the outbreak of the Second World War but played most of his football for the Molineux club during the wartime Leagues. In 1946 he signed for Bournemouth and helped the Dean Court club to win the Third Division (South) Cup, scoring the winning goal in the final. After having scored 57 goals for the Cherries, McDonald joined Fulham in the summer of 1948 and made his début in a 3–2 win at Grimsby Town on the opening day of the 1948–49 season. He missed just one game in his first campaign with the Cottagers as the club went on to win the Second Division title. Midway through the 1949–50 season he suffered from a series of injuries and a loss of form and was never quite the same player. He had scored 20 goals in 78 games when he left Craven Cottage in August 1952 to join Southampton. Things didn't work out for him at The Dell and nine months later he moved to Southend United where he ended his League career. He had a spell playing non-League football for Weymouth before hanging up his boots.

McINTYRE, JAMES James McIntyre appeared for Walsall, Notts County, Northampton, Reading and Coventry City before hanging up his boots. He went to work in the Humber car factory before spending a season refereeing in the North Warwickshire League. In 1907 he returned to Highfield Road as the club's assistant trainer. Within a matter of months he had become Coventry's chief trainer, a position he held for five months before moving to The Dell as Southampton's trainer. During the First World War he worked in a munitions factory but on his return to Southampton in 1919 he was appointed the club's manager. He was still in charge when the club entered the Football League and in 1921–22 led them to the Third Division (South) Championship. Two years later he left the club to run a hotel in Scotland. Coventry City managed to persuade him back as their manager but he left Highfield Road in April 1931 to manage Fulham. In his first full season in charge, 1931–32, he led the Cottagers to the Third Division (South) title, the first manager to achieve this feat twice with different clubs. The following season the club just missed out on promotion to the First Division, finishing in third place in Division Two. McIntyre then inexplicably sold 'Bonzo' Newton, the club's leading goalscorer in these two seasons, to Reading, a decision which ultimately led to his dismissal in February 1934 following a run of poor results.

McNABB, JOCK The brother of Scottish international wing-half John McNabb, he was playing in the Lanarkshire Junior League when Portsmouth offered him the chance to play League football in 1923. He had made just nine appearances for Pompey when Fulham manager Andy Ducat persuaded him to come to Craven Cottage in the summer of 1925. The tough-tackling centre-half made his Fulham děbut in a 2–2 draw at Barnsley in October of that year after which he missed very few games over the next five seasons. Though much of that time was spent with the Cottagers struggling to avoid relegation from the Second Division – the club eventually dropped into the Third Division (South) in 1927–28 – McNabb captained the side with great enthusiasm. He enjoyed nothing more than joining his forwards in attack and in 169 League and Cup games scored 21 goals, mainly from set pieces, before leaving to play for Coventry City. His stay at Highfield Road was brief and he ended his career with Llanelli, playing with the Welsh club for five seasons before retiring.

MACDONALD, MALCOLM Malcom Macdonald began his football career as a full-back with Tonbridge before joining Fulham in August 1968. Manager Bobby Robson switched him to centre-forward and in 1968–69, his only season with the club, he scored five goals in 13 games. When Robson left, Macdonald fell out of favour and was transferred to Luton Town for £30,000 in the summer of 1969. In two seasons with the Hatters he averaged well over a goal every other game, scoring 49 goals in 88 League games. Eventually Newcastle United signed him for £180,000 in May 1971. On Tyneside he became the greatest idol since the days of Jackie Milburn. In one of his first matches for the Magpies, he scored a hat-trick against Liverpool and finished each of his five seasons with Newcastle as the leading scorer, totalling 138 goals in 258 games. He scored five goals in one match for England – against Cyprus – to equal the individual scoring record. He also scored in every round of the FA Cup when Newcastle reached the FA Cup final in 1973–74. When Arsenal paid £333,333 for his services in August 1976, the whole of Tyneside was stunned. In his first season at Highbury, he was the First Division's leading goalscorer. In 1977–78 he helped Arsenal to the FA Cup final against Ipswich Town but after just four games of the following season he suffered a serious leg injury in a League Cup tie at Rotherham United. In July 1979, at the age of 29, Malcolm Macdonald announced his retirement. In a little over two seasons at Highbury, Macdonald scored 57 goals in 107 League and Cup games. He returned to Craven Cottage as the club's marketing executive, later being appointed manager as successor to Bobby Campbell. In his first few months in charge, he steered the club clear of relegation to the Fourth Division and in 1981–82 he led the club to promotion to Division Two. The following season he almost took the Cottagers into the top-flight but in 1983–84 the team began to struggle and in March 1984, following revelations about his private life, he left Craven Cottage to run a pub in Worthing. Macdonald returned to football as manager of Huddersfield Town in 1987–88.

Malcolm Macdonald

MACEDO, TONY The son of a famous Barcelona and Spanish international footballer, goalkeeper Tony Macedo was born in Gibraltar; his family moved to England when he was only two years old. On leaving school, Macedo became an apprentice cabinet-maker but in 1954 he joined Fulham's ground-staff. Despite signing professional forms in 1956, his League début was delayed by National Service. His first-team début came on 7 December 1957 when the Cottagers paid his air fare from his RAF base in Germany and flew him to the match at Bristol City where he replaced the injured Ian Black. Macedo kept a clean sheet in a 5–0 win and held his place as the club's first-choice keeper for the next ten seasons. In 1958–59 he helped Fulham win promotion to the First Division, his form during the campaign leading to him winning the first of ten England Under-23 caps when he played against Italy. Yet despite playing behind England international full-backs George Cohen and Jim Langley, Macedo never gained the full international recognition that his performances deserved. Towards the end of his career at Craven Cottage, a series of niggling injuries restricted his first-team appearances and in the summer of 1968, after playing in 391 League and Cup games for the Cottagers, he left to join Colchester United. After just one season with the Layer Road club, in which he made 39 appearances, he left to live in South Africa.

MACKAY, DON Goalkeeper Don Mackay began his career with Forfar Athletic, was transferred to Dundee United in 1969 and made 49 League appearances for them before trying his luck in England with Southend United. When his playing days were over he turned his attention to coaching and worked with Bristol City before accepting the manager's job at Dens Park, the home of Dundee. After four years of success, he was given the job at Coventry City. He staved off relegation twice but, in April 1986, he was dismissed. He returned to Scotland to run the reserve and youth sides for Graeme Souness at Rangers until, in February 1987, he was appointed manager of Blackburn Rovers. He steered the Ewood Park club to a Full Members' Cup victory at Wembley and brought in big name players like Archibald, Ardiles, Stapleton and Moran. Having taken the Lancashire club to the brink of the top-flight on three successive occasions, he was sacked after just three games of the 1991–92 season. Mackay's arrival at Fulham as manager in January 1992 saw a steady improvement in results which ended with the club just missing out on the play-offs. However, following the club's relegation to the Third Division in 1993–94, he was sacked.

MANAGERS In nearly 100 years, Fulham FC have had 26 full-time managers, as follows:

Harry Bradshaw	1904–1909	Bill Dodgin Jnr	1969–1972

Phil Kelso	1909–1924	Alec Stock	1972–76
Andy Ducat	1924–26	Bobby Campbell	1976–1980
Joe Bradshaw	1926–29	Malcolm Macdonald	1980–84
Ned Liddell	1929–1931	Ray Harford	1984–86
James McIntyre	1931–34	Ray Lewington	1986–1990
Jimmy Hogan	1934–35	Alan Dicks	1990–91
Jack Peart	1935–1948	Don Mackay	1991–949
Frank Osborne*	1948–1964	Ian Branfoot**	1994–6
Bill Dodgin Snr	1949–1953	Micky Adams	1996–97
Duggie Livingstone	1956–58	Ray Wilkins	1997–98
Bedford Jezzard	1958–1964	Kevin Keegan***	1998–99
Vic Buckingham	1965–68	Paul Bracewell	1999–2000
Bobby Robson	1968	Jean Tigana	2000

* was Secretary-Manager or General Manager for much of this period.

** continued as General Manager

*** Chief Operating Officer

MARATHON MATCHES One Cottagers' Cup match – the fourth-round tie against Nottingham Forest in 1974–75 – went to four games: Neither side could score in the first meeting at Craven Cottage whilst a John Dowie goal in the replay at the City Ground helped Fulham draw 1–1. The third meeting at Craven Cottage also ended all-square at 1–1, Alan Slough netting Fulham's goal. The tie was eventually settled at the fourth attempt when Fulham won 2–1 at Forest with Viv Busby scoring both the club's goals. The club have been involved in a number of ties that went to three meetings: Reading (League Cup 1972–73), Hull City (FA Cup 1974–75), Bolton Wanderers

(League Cup 1976–77), Bury (FA Cup 1980–81) and Liverpool (League Cup 1983–84).

MARKSMEN – LEAGUE Fulham's top League scorer is Gordon Davies, who struck 159 goals during his two spells with the club. Only six players have hit more than 100 League goals for the club.

1	Gordon Davies	159
2	Bedford Jezzard	154
3	Johnny Haynes	146
4	Jim Hammond	141
5	Graham Leggatt	127
6	Arthur Stevens	110
7	Steve Earle	98
8	Maurice Cook	89
9=	Frank Newton	77
	Bobby Robson	77

MARKSMEN – OVERALL Gordon Davies is the club's top marksman with 178 goals. Only seven players have scored over 100 goals for the club:

1	Gordon Davies	178
2	Johnny Haynes	157
3	Bedford Jezzard	154
4	Jim Hammond	150
5	Graham Leggatt	134
6	Arthur Stevens	124
7	Steve Earle	108

MARSH, RODNEY Rodney Marsh began his career with Fulham, scoring a superb volleyed goal on his début as the Cottagers beat Aston Villa 1–0 in March 1963. After playing in just a handful of games over the next two seasons, he established himself in the Fulham side in 1964–65, scoring 17 goals in 41 games. In February 1965, Marsh sustained a serious injury in the 5–1 defeat at Leicester City, an injury which left him partially deaf. Midway through the following season, Marsh lost form and was transferred to Queen's Park Rangers for £15,000. He played an important role in Rangers' rise from the Third to the First Division, winning a Third Division Championship medal in 1966–67. He also won a League Cup winners' medal whilst at Loftus Road, scoring one of the goals in a 3–2 win over West Bromwich Albion. In March 1972, Manchester City paid £200,000 to bring Marsh to Maine Road. With Marsh in the side, City became a joy to watch as his imaginative play set up a host of chances for his team-mates. Though not a prolific scorer, he did manage one hat-trick for the club in the 4–1 defeat of York City in the 1973–74 League Cup competition, and won a runners-up medal when City lost 2–1 to Wolves in the final. Marsh then moved to the United States to play for Tampa Bay Rowdies before returning to Craven Cottage to team up with George Best. Sadly for Marsh and the Fulham faithful, injury dogged his stay and after scoring 28 goals in 90 games he was forced to retire.

MARSHALL, ALFRED Darlington-born half-back Alfred Marshall played his early football for his local clubs, St John's and St Augustine's, before Fulham manager Phil Kelso brought him to Craven Cottage in September 1909. He had to wait five months before making his first-team début in a 3–0 defeat at Bradford. Over the next three seasons, Marshall made just 20 League appearances and it was 1912–13 before he established himself as a first-team regular. Unfortunately for Marshall, he was at the peak of his career when the First World War broke out and he played in just three games in 1914–15 after being called up. He returned to the Fulham side in 1919–20 and had taken his total of League and Cup appearances to 107 when he was allowed to join First Division Oldham Athletic. He had spent three seasons with the Boundary Park club, appearing in 66 League games when, in June 1923, he collapsed at his home in Darlington and died aged 35.

MARSHALL, JOHN One of the club's longest-serving players, John

Rodney Marsh

Marshall played in virtually every position for the Cottagers (except goal) after joining the club as an apprentice in the summer of 1982. He made his League début for Fulham in a 2–0 defeat at home to Portsmouth in September 1983 after which he was a regular member of the Cottagers' side for fifteen seasons. Marshall could always be relied upon to produce a thoroughly professional display, no matter what position he was asked to play in. A good all-

John Marshall

rounder, he broke a leg in the 1–0 home win over Gillingham in April 1995 and, though many thought it would be the end of his career, he battled back to full fitness and returned to the side midway through the 1995–96 season. At the end of that campaign, he took over the coaching of Fulham's youth team as well as adding his great experience to the club's Capital League side. His only first-team experience in that season was in the second leg of the League Cup tie at Ipswich Town, taking his total of League and Cup appearances (in which he has scored 33 goals) to 465.

MATCH OF THE DAY Fulham's first appearance on BBC's Match of the Day was on 5 September 1964 when they beat Manchester United 2–1 at Craven Cottage with an own goal by Nobby Stiles and a Johnny Haynes special.

MATTHEWSON, REG Sheffield-born centre-half Reg Matthewson began his career with his home-town team, Sheffield United, playing his first game for the Blades at Craven Cottage on 17 March 1962. It wasn't the best of débuts. Matthewson was led a merry dance by Maurice Cook, who netted a hat-trick in a 5–2 win for the Cottagers. Matthewson went on to play in 149 League games for the Yorkshire club before joining Fulham in February 1968 for a fee of £30,000. He made his Fulham début in a 4–3 home win over Burnley after which he missed very few games for the Craven Cottage club. He helped them win promotion to the Second Division in 1970–71, a campaign in which he scored his only goal for the club in a 4–0 home win over Torquay United. Following the arrival of Paul Went from Charlton Athletic, Matthewson, who had appeared in 174 League and Cup games, lost his place and left to play for Chester City. He appeared for the Cestrians in 87 League games before spells as player-coach of Bangor City and assistant manager of Shrewsbury Town.

MAVIN, FRED Fred Mavin began his career with his home-town team of Newcastle United but, unable to break into the first-team, came south to play for New Brompton. He made 115 appearances for the Kent side before leaving to join Fulham in the summer of 1909. He made his début for the Craven Cottage club in a 2–0 win at Stockport County on the opening day of the 1909–10 season, going on to be a first-team regular for the next four seasons. Appointed club captain, he scored 10 goals from his position of centre-half in seasons 1910–11 and 1911–12, a record for a defender that stood at Fulham for seventy years. He had scored 27 goals in 149 League and Cup games when in December 1913 he left to play for Bradford. During the First World War he 'guested' for Fulham, making 39 appearances before later playing for Reading. A serious injury brought his playing career to an end and, after a spell managing Exeter City, he took charge of Crystal Palace just after their entry into the League. In 1928–29 he led the Selhurst Park club to runners-up in the Third Division (South) behind Charlton Athletic on goal average. He ended his involvement in the game after managing his old club Gillingham.

MELLOR, PETER After impressing for both Manchester and Lancashire Schoolboys, goalkeeper Peter Mellor was given a trial with Manchester United but was discarded and crossed the city to become an apprentice at Maine Road. Although he won an England Youth cap in 1966, he was unable to break into City's first-team and joined Witton Albion of the Cheshire League in 1968. In April 1969, Burnley paid £1,750 for his services and in his first season with the club he was ever-present. However, in the close season, he suffered a shoulder injury and was out of action until November 1970. When he returned, he was subjected to constant barracking by a section of the home fans and, after a loan spell with Chesterfield, he signed for Fulham in February

Peter Mellor

1972. He made his début for the Cottagers in a 2–0 home win over Bristol City after which he was a virtual ever-present at Craven Cottage until 1976. He spent all his time at Fulham in Division Two but he excelled in Fulham's run to an FA Cup final appearance at Wembley in 1975. Mellor's luck deserted him on the big day and the Cottagers went down to a brace of goals from West Ham's Alan Taylor. The beginning of the end of Peter Mellor's Craven Cottage career came in November 1976 when he was injured during a heavy defeat by Notts County. Mellor, who had played in 224 games for Fulham, never appeared for the Cottagers again, leaving for Hereford United early the following season. He later joined Portsmouth and, after a respectable first season at Fratton Park, helped Pompey to win promotion to the Third Division in 1979–80 before retiring two years later. Peter Mellor now lives in Florida where he has prospered selling and fitting fireplaces as well as maintaining gardens and swimming pools. He is the Florida state goalkeeping coach and coaches goalkeepers throughout the States.

MITCHELL, JOHN John Mitchell was playing for his home-town team St Albans City when Fulham spotted his potential and signed him for a fee of £3,000 in February 1972. He made his début in a 1–1 draw against Huddersfield Town early the following season and ended the campaign with 11 goals in 36 outings. Unable to maintain this early promise due to a loss of form and a series of niggling injuries, he spent most of the next two seasons in the club's reserve side. However, he did return for the latter stages of the club's FA Cup run in 1975 and scored in both semi-final matches against Birmingham City including the winner at Maine Road which took the Cottagers to Wembley for the first time in their history. Unfortunately he couldn't find the net in the final which Fulham lost 2-0 to West Ham United. In 1976–77, Mitchell was the club's leading scorer with 20 goals in 38 games including four in a 6–1 home win over Orient. He continued to find the net with great regularity and the following season netted a hat-trick in a 5–1 defeat of Notts County. He had scored 61 goals in 194 games for the Cottagers when in June 1978 he was surprisingly allowed to join Millwall for £100,000. His progress at the Den was hampered by injuries and in four seasons he had scored 18 goals in 81 League games when he was forced to retire. After a spell as manager of St Albans, he made a takeover bid for Luton Town but now runs a marketing and promotions company in London's West End.

MITTEN, CHARLIE Charlie Mitten was born in Rangoon, Burma where his father was serving with the Royal Scots Guards. He later lived in Scotland where he played junior football for Strathallen Hawthorne and Dunblane Rovers before joining Manchester United in 1936. However, he had to wait until after the Second World War before making his League début and during the hostilities, he 'guested' for Aston Villa, Chelsea, Southampton and Tranmere Rovers. After the war he went straight into the United side and was always first choice. In March 1950 he became only the second player to score a hat-trick of penalties as United beat Aston Villa 7–0 – in fact, he scored four goals for United that day! Ironically they were to be the last he scored for the Old Trafford club because in June of that year, Mitten, along with a number of other leading professionals, quit the English game and signed for the Colombian side Sante Fe. Mitten had been promised huge sums of money, much of which never materialised, and it wasn't long before he was on the plane back home. Matt Busby refused to have him back and Mitten was immediately placed on the transfer list. In January 1952, Mitten joined Fulham, making his début in a 2–1 home defeat by Chelsea. Despite scoring six times in 16 games in that 1951–52 season, he couldn't prevent the Cottagers from being relegated. One of the most exciting players of his generation, he had scored 33 goals in 160 games when he left Craven Cottage in 1956 to become player-manager of Mansfield Town. He later had a successful spell as manager of Newcastle United but in 1961 he ended his involvement with the game and returned to Manchester to manage the White City greyhound stadium.

MONEY, RICHARD Utility player Richard Money began his Football League career with Scunthorpe United and had made 179 appearances for the Irons when Fulham manager Bobby Campbell paid £50,000 to bring him to Craven Cottage in December 1977. Money made his Fulham début in a 2–0 home win over Bolton Wanderers after which he missed very few games, being ever-present in 1978–79. At the end of the following season, Money, who had scored four goals in 115 game,s was transferred to Liverpool for a club record incoming transfer fee of £333,333. Money, who had gained recognition by England at 'B' and Under-23 international level, never really established himself at Anfield. Good in the air and comfortable on the ball, he left the Reds and signed for Luton Town for £100,000 in April 1982. A year later he joined Portsmouth but a broken leg hampered his progress and in October 1985 he returned to his first club, Scunthorpe, before becoming a coach.

Richard Money

MOORE, BOBBY Bobby Moore was the first captain to lift three trophies at Wembley Stadium in three consecutive years. He lifted the FA Cup in 1964, the European Cup Winners' Cup in 1965 (both with West Ham United) and the World Cup in 1966. He played a record 18 times for England Youth, turned professional in June 1958 and followed the conventional route towards the international team with eight Under-23 caps and an international début in Peru in May 1962. After 17 caps, Moore was made England's youngest-ever captain for the match against Czechoslovakia in May 1963. In 1964, West Ham won the FA Cup,

Bobby Moore

beating Preston North End 3–2 in the final, and Moore was elected Footballer of the Year. Cup victory sent the Hammers into Europe and the following season they beat TSV Munich 1860 in one of the finest performances by a British side in Europe. Moore grew immeasurably during these two seasons. His leadership of West Ham had established his place as one of the most influential people in the British game. He was now in the front rank of international defenders, his natural ability refined by Ron Greenwood and his England manager Alf Ramsey. If the England side of 1966 was steeped in the dogma of Ramsey, it was inspired by the example of Moore. He won the Player of Players award at the end of the tournament and actually became a better player in the seasons which followed the 1966 triumph. His distribution of the ball was impeccable, he was able to use it constructively from deep positions. Alongside this, he was one of the best readers of the game, having an uncanny knack of always appearing to know what his opponent was going to do. In March 1974, after appearing in 642 games for the Hammers, he joined Fulham and made his début against Middlesbrough, a match the Cottagers lost 4-0! Moore missed very few games over the next four seasons and in 1975 inspired the Cottagers to reach the FA Cup final at Wembley where they lost 2-0 to West Ham United. Moore, whose only goal for Fulham came against Crystal Palace in April 1974, appeared in 150 games before hanging up his boots. After breaking Bobby Charlton's England appearance record, he played only one more game for his country. The whole country mourned when Bobby Moore died of cancer in 1993.

Simon Morgan

MORGAN, SIMON Birmingham-born Simon Morgan began his Football League career with Leicester City where his performances made England Under-21 honours an inevitability. Sadly, most of his time at Filbert Street saw him suffer lengthy injury problems and in October 1990, after scoring four goals in 182 games, he was transferred to Fulham for £100,000. He made his début for the Cottagers in a 2–1 defeat at Stoke City and scored his first goal for the club on his home début as Bury were beaten 2–0. He was soon made captain at Craven Cottage, leading the side by example. He helped the club win promotion to the Second Division in 1996–97 when, in the only two games he missed through injury, the Cottagers failed to score! Originally a defender, Morgan moved into midfield where his driving force and ability to score spectacular goals made him a great favourite with the Fulham fans. A bad injury midway through the 1997–98 season caused him to lose the captaincy to Paul Bracewell but in 1998–99 he was back to his best playing alongside Kit Symons and Chris Coleman as Fulham won their first divisional championship for fifty years. One of the longest-serving players at Craven Cottage, Simon Morgan has now scored 57 goals in 386 games for Fulham.

MORRISON, BILLY Billy Morrison began his career with West Calder FC before playing in the Scottish League for St Bernards. His performances attracted clubs south of the border and in the summer of 1904 Morrison joined Fulham. One of a number of Scots signed by manager Harry Bradshaw, he made a goalscoring début for the Cottagers, netting in a 1–1 draw at home to New Brompton. That season the towering centre-half was instrumental in the club reaching the FA Cup quarter-finals where they lost 5–0 to the eventual winners, Aston Villa, having helped keep seven clean sheets in the previous games in the competition. Morrison won two Southern League Championship medals before going on to make his Football League début against Hull City in the club's inaugural game in the competition. He went on to play in 31 League games before losing his place to George Parsonage and left to join Glossop, the club against whom he made his last appearance for Fulham. After two seasons with Glossop, Morrison joined Raith Rovers and after helping them reach the Scottish Cup final, where they lost to Falkirk, he left Stark's Park at the outbreak of the First World War.

MOST MATCHES Fulham played their greatest number of matches in season 1974–75 when they played 66. This comprised of 42 League games, 12 FA Cup games, three League Cup games, and nine Anglo-Scottish Cup games when they reached the final only to lose 1–0 on aggregate to Middlesbrough.

MULLERY, ALAN Within two months of signing for Fulham as a 17-year-old professional, wing-half Alan Mullery had made his League début in a 5–2 home win over Leyton Orient in February 1959. He appeared in the last 14 games of the season, helping the Cottagers win promotion to the First Division. A permanent member of the Fulham side, his impressive performances in the top-flight led to him winning the first of his three England Under-23 caps when he played against Italy in November 1960. Mullery had appeared in 218 games for the Cottagers when, in March 1964, Spurs paid £72,500 for his services. Two months later he played for the Football League against the Italian League

Alan Mullery

and, after one more outing with the Football League, won his first full cap against Holland in December of that year. Restricted at international level by the performances of Nobby Stiles, he did not win his second cap until May 1967, four days after winning an FA Cup winners' medal against Chelsea. After that he became an England regular, winning 33 more caps. In 1968 he became club captain and led Spurs to victory in the 1971 League Cup final. However, in October of that year he began to suffer from a deep-seated pelvic strain which put him out of action for six months. On recovery, he went on loan to Fulham but after a month was recalled owing to a lengthy injury list at White Hart Lane. Leading the club into their UEFA Cup semi-final with AC Milan, he clinched the tie with a brilliant 20-yard volley at the San Siro Stadium before going on to secure the trophy with a header – he knocked himself out in the process – in the second leg of the final against Wolves. He returned to Craven Cottage in the close season of 1972 for a fee of £65,000 after appearing in 429 games for Spurs. In 1975 he won an FA Cup runners-up medal after the Cottagers had been beaten 2–0 by West Ham United. Mullery, who had been made skipper by manager Alec Stock was elected Footballer of the Year and awarded the MBE. He had scored 42 goals in 412 games for Fulham when he hung up his boots and went into management with Brighton, leading them from the Third to the First Division before moving to Charlton. He spent only a year with the Addicks before managing Crystal Palace and Queen's Park Rangers for two years each and then finishing his career with another spell at Brighton.

N

NEUTRAL GROUNDS Whilst Craven Cottage housed the England v Wales international in 1907 and has been used on a number of occasions as a venue for FA Cup replays, the Cottagers themselves have had to replay on a neutral ground in the FA Cup four times – Manchester United at Villa Park in 1904–05; Reading at White Hart Lane in 1904–05; Hull City at Filbert Street in 1974–75 and Bury at the Hawthorns in 1980–81. The club also had to replay against Bolton Wanderers at St Andrew's in a League Cup tie in 1976–77. The club's involvement in the Test Matches in seasons 1899–1900, 1901–02 and 1902–03 were also played on neutral grounds. The club's FA Cup semi-finals were of course played on neutral grounds with the following results:

Date	*Opponents*	*Venue*	*Score*
28.03 1908	Newcastle United	Anfield	0–6
21.03 1936	Sheffield United	Molineux	1–2
22.03 1958	Manchester United	Villa Park	2–2
26.03 1958	Manchester United	Highbury	3–5
31.03 1962	Burnley	Villa Park	1–1

09.04 1962	Burnley	Filbert Street	1–2
05.04 1975	Birmingham City	Hillsborough	1–1
09.04 1975	Birmingham City	Maine Road	1–0

Fulham's FA Cup final appearance at Wembley in 1975 also qualifies for inclusion.

NEWTON, FRANK After leaving the army, Frank Newton joined non-League Ashton United from where he signed for Stockport County in January 1928. After making his League début in a 4–1 defeat at Ashington two months later, he found that for the next season or so his opportunities were limited by the presence of Harry Burgess and Joe Smith, though he did score 16 goals in 19 League games in 1928–29. Before the start of the following season, Burgess had joined Sheffield Wednesday and Joe Smith had retired, so it was Newton who partnered new signing Andy Lincoln. Newton went on to score 36 goals in 35 League appearances including five goals in a 6-1 win over Nelson, four in a 6–1 defeat of Rotherham United and all three in a 3–0 victory over Doncaster Rovers. Remarkably, in early January, after scoring 21 goals in the first 22 matches of the season, he was dropped! In 1930–31, 'Bonzo' Newton, as he was known, scored 34 goals in 39 League games including hat-tricks against Gateshead (home 3–1) and Lincoln City (home 4–2). After scoring 93 goals in only 101 games, he left Edgeley Park but surprisingly joined another Third Division team in Fulham. He scored twice on his début as the Cottagers beat Coventry City 5–3 on the opening day of the 1931–32 season and ended the campaign in which the club won the Third Division (South) Championship as Fulham's leading scorer with 43 goals – still a club record. Included in this total were hat–tricks in the games against Exeter City (away 3–0) Coventry City (away 5–5) and Luton Town (away 3–1). He continued to form a prolific goalscoring partnership with Jim Hammond and was the club's leading scorer in their first season back in Division Two. In September 1933 he joined Reading but within a year he was back with Fulham. He had scored 81 goals in just 88 games for the Cottagers when his return to the club took a cruel twist, the player breaking his leg in a friendly only two months after he had re-signed. At the age of 32 and having scored an incredible 192 goals in 209 League appearances for his three clubs, 'Bonzo' Newton's career was over.

NICKNAMES Fulham's nickname is the Cottagers, in reference to the side's home at Craven Cottage. Many players in the club's history have also been known fondly by their nickname. They include:

Ted Charlton	1906–1920	Taffa
Herbert Kingaby	1906–1907	Rabbit
Alfred Marshall	1910–1920	Rubberneck
Syd Gibbons	1930–1938	Carnera
Alf Tootill	1932–1938	The Birdcatcher
Gordon Brice	1952–1956	Whiz
Fred Callaghan	1962–1973	Tank
Allan Clarke	1966–1968	Sniffer
Sean O'Driscoll	1979–1983	Noisey

NON-LEAGUE Non-League is the shorthand term for clubs which are not members of the Football League. The Cottagers have a mixed record against non-League opposition in the FA Cup competition. The club's record since the Second World War is:

Date	*Opponents*	*Stage*	*Venue*	*Score*
04.01 1958	Yeovil Town	Round 3	Home	4–0
10.01 1959	Peterborough United	Round 3	Home	0–0
24.01 1959	Peterborough United	Round 3	Away	1–0
27.01 1968	Macclesfield Town	Round 3	Home	4–2
18.11 1989	Bath City	Round 1	Away	2–2
21.11 1989	Bath City	Round 1R	Home	2–1
17.11 1990	Farnborough Town	Round 1	Home	2–1

15.11	1991	Hayes	Round 1	Home	0–2
15.11	1993	Yeovil Town	Round 1	Away	0–1
11.11	1994	Ashford	Round 1	Away	2–2
22.11	1994	Ashford	Round 1R	Home	5–3
16.11	1997	Margate	Round 1	Away	2–1
13.11	1998	Leigh RMI	Round 1	Home	1–1
23.11	1998	Leigh RMI	Round 1R	Away	2–0

O

O'CALLAGHAN, TAFFY The star of Tottenham Hotspur's forward line throughout the late 1920s and early 1930s, O'Callaghan was working in the pits when invited to join the club's groundstaff in 1925. A clever player who packed a good shot in either foot, he scored plenty of goals for the club. After making his début against Everton in February 1927, replacing the injured Jimmy Seed, he soon became a great favourite with the White Hart Lane crowd. In fact, he did so well that Seed was unable to regain his place and eventually left the club to join Sheffield Wednesday. O'Callaghan continued to go from strength to strength and made his first appearance for Wales against Northern Ireland in May 1929. He won 11 full caps in his time with Spurs and scored twice when Wales beat Scotland 5–2 in October 1932. Having helped Spurs to promotion in 1932–33 he was surprisingly transferred to Leicester City in March 1935 when the White Hart Lane club were struggling to avoid relegation. O'Callaghan, who had scored 98 goals in 263 games for Spurs, won a Second Division Championship medal with the Filbert Street side in 1936–37 before moving to Fulham early the following season. He made his début for the Cottagers in a 3-1 home win over his first club, Spurs, having a hand in all Fulham's goals. He was a regular member of the Fulham side in 1937–38 but the following season he was hampered by injuries. He appeared in 33 wartime games for the club, playing his last match for the Cottagers in the 1945–46 season. He then joined the Craven Cottage club's training staff, working with the reserves until his death in July 1956.

O'CONNELL, PAT Pat O'Connell made his début for Fulham at inside-right in the 4–1 defeat at Stoke City in December 1958 but over the next seven seasons he showed his versatility by playing at outside-left and in both full-back positions. Though not a prolific goalscorer, his best season was 1960–61 when he netted ten goals in 26 games, though he did provide numerous goalscoring opportunities for the likes of Graham Leggatt and Rodney Marsh. He had scored 28 goals in 170 first-team outings for the Cottagers when in July 1966 he left to play for Crystal Palace. After one season at Selhurst Park, in which he made 21 League appearances, he went to play for Vancouver who were at the time managed by the great Hungarian international Ferenc Puskas. On returning to these shores, he joined non-League Brentwood and in 1969–70 helped them reach the third-round of the FA Cup. He later had spells with Dover, Wimbledon and Epsom and Ewell, for whom he appeared in the FA Vase final at Wembley before becoming their manager.

O'DRISCOLL, SEAN Born in Wolverhampton of Irish parents, midfielder Sean O'Driscoll played his early football for non-League Alvechurch before Fulham manager Bobby Campbell paid £12,000 for his services in November 1979. He made his Fulham début four months later against Bristol Rovers after which he was a first-team regular for four seasons. An ever-present in seasons 1981–82 and 1982–83, he helped the Cottagers win promotion to the Second Division in the first of those seasons. His form led to him winning three full caps for the Republic of Ireland, the first against Chile in Santiago in May 1982. He went on to score 13 goals in 173 League and Cup games before being transferred to Bournemouth for £6,000 in May 1983, following an earlier loan spell. He helped the Cherries win the Associate Members' Cup in 1984 and the Third Division Championship in 1986–87. He went on to score 24 goals in 511 games for the Dean Court club before becoming their physiotherapist.

OLDEST PLAYER The oldest player to line-up in a Fulham team is Walter White. He was 40 years 275 days old when he played the last of his 203 first-team games for the club against Bury in February 1923, a match the Cottagers won 1–0.

OLIVER, LEN Len Oliver began his career with Isthmian League side Tufnell Park before Fulham manager Andy Ducat secured his services in the summer of 1924. The strong-tackling half-back went into the Cottagers' side, making his début in a 5–1 defeat at Derby County. He was a first-team regular for the next eleven seasons, missing very few games and being an ever-present in 1926–27, 1928–29 and 1932–33. Oliver captained the Cottagers for seven seasons and in 1931–32 led the side to their first-ever promotion as champions of the Third Division (South). His performances for Fulham whilst they were in the Third Division led to him becoming one of the few players from that League to win full international honours when he played for England against Belgium in 1929. Oliver went on to play in 434 League and Cup games for Fulham, his two goals coming against Walsall (home 5–1 in 1928–29) and Southend United (away 4–2 in 1930–31) before he lost his place following the appointment of Jimmy Hogan as manager. He left Craven Cottage in 1937 to coach Cliftonville but on the outbreak of the Second World War he became a physical training instructor. After the hostilities had ended, he returned to coaching with Arlesey Town.

OSBORNE, FRANK Frank Osborne was born in South Africa where his father was a colonel in the Royal Army Medical Corps and returned with his family to England in 1911. He joined the well-known amateur club Bromley in 1913 and within two years was playing the professional game. Osborne scored on his Fulham début in a 4–1 win at Sheffield Wednesday in November 1921, going on to score 18 goals in 70 games for the Cottagers. He won two England caps whilst at Craven Cottage, showing his versatility by operating at centre-forward against Ireland in October 1922 and at outside-right against France in May 1923. Slightly built, Osborne could ably fill any of the forward positions. His accurate passing and shrewd positional sense prompted Spurs to pay £1,500 for his services in January 1924. He won two more England caps whilst with Spurs, scoring a hat-trick in the second of these as Belgium were beaten 5–3. Despite his fine scoring record when played at centre-forward, he did not fill that role often enough and this probably prevented him collecting more international honours than he did. With age catching up on him, Osborne, who had scored 87 goals in 228 games for Spurs, left to join Southampton. He stayed at The Dell for two years before retiring. Appointed a director at Fulham in 1935, he stepped down from the board to take over as team manager in September 1948 and in his first season led the Cottagers to the Second Division title. Though the club were relegated in 1952, Osborne took them back up to the First Division in 1959 and served the club for sixteen years as team manager, general manager and secretary-manager before retiring.

OVERSEAS PLAYERS Canadian international Paul Peschisolido joined Fulham from West Bromwich Albion for £1.1 million in October 1997. The prolific goalscorer netted a hat-trick in a 5–0 defeat of Carlisle United, to help the Cottagers reach the play-offs where he was sent off in the second leg against Grimsby Town. Switched to a deeper role following the signings of Horsfield and Hayles, Peschisolido helped the club win the Second Division title in 1998–99. South African international goalkeeper Andre Arendse joined the Cottagers from Capetown Spurs but due to the fine form of Northern Ireland international keeper Maik Taylor, his appearances have been limited. Gus Uhlenbeek joined Fulham from Ipswich Town under the Bosman ruling in the summer of 1998. The Surinam-born winger won a Second Division Championship medal in his first season with the club although more than half his appearances were as a substitute. Dirk Lehmann cost £30,000 from German Second Division club Cottbus, but after scoring five goals in 35 outings in 1998–99, he was released and joined Hibernian. Francois Keller was signed from Strasbourg in December 1998 but his only first-team start was in the Auto Windscreen Shield tie at Torquay United. Belgian international Philippe Albert joined the Cottagers on loan from Newcastle United in January 1999, helping them win the Second Division Championship after appearing in a variety of positions.

OWN GOALS Whilst there have been a number of instances of own goals scored by Fulham players, none can compare with the ones scored by Frank Elliott and Alan Mullery. In the Second Division game between Plymouth Argyle and Fulham at Home Park on 2 October 1954, Frank Elliott the Fulham keeper, in trying to cut out a centre-cum-shot, was challenged in mid-air by Argyle centre-forward Langman. Elliott fell to the ground injured. The ball rolled loose, but unaware of his position in relation to the goal, he grabbed the ball and threw it over his head and into the unguarded net. Plymouth Argyle won 3–2! Only thirty seconds had been played of the disastrous 6–1 home defeat by Sheffield Wednesday on 21 January 1961 when Mullery contrived to score an own goal past Tony Macedo without a Wednesday player touching the ball!

P

PARKER, PAUL Paul Parker began his career with Fulham and, after progressing through the club's youth side, he made his Football League début in a 2–1 home defeat by Reading in April 1981, whilst still an apprentice. He duly turned professional a year later but it wasn't until 1983–84 that he began to hold down a regular place in the side. Parker, who won England Youth honours in 1981, represented England at Under-21 level on eight occasions. At the end of the 1985–86 season, however, Fulham were relegated to the Third Division and although he remained at the club during the following season, it was obvious that he deserved a higher class of football. He had scored three goals in 181 League and Cup games when in June 1987 he joined Queen's Park Rangers for £300,000. Ever-present throughout his first season at Loftus Road, Parker was rewarded for his consistent displays with his first full cap against Albania. He had an impressive World Cup in 1990 but at the end of the following season, after he had played in 160 games, he was transferred to Manchester United for £2 million. During his time at Old Trafford, Parker, who went on to play 19 times for England, won two Premier League Championship medals, an FA Cup winners' medal and a League Cup winners' medal. Sadly injuries restricted his number of appearances and in five years with the club he only played in 135 League and Cup games. After being given a free transfer, he had spells with Derby County and Sheffield United before rejoining Fulham for three League games prior to ending his first-class career with Chelsea.

Paul Parker

PEARCE, HERBERT Prolific goalscoring centre-forward Herbert Pearce had a very successful non-League career with Wanstead, Ilford and Leytonstone before joining Second Division Fulham in April 1911. After making his début in a 1–0 defeat at Bristol City on the opening day of the 1911–12 season, Pearce went on to establish a new club goalscoring record with 21 goals in 34 League games. Included in his total were hat-tricks in the wins over Leeds City (home 7–2) and Leicester Fosse (home 4–1). He netted another hat-trick the following season as

Stockport County were beaten 7–0 at Craven Cottage, his form leading to him playing for the South v North in a full international trial. Pearce, who also topped the club's scoring charts in 1913–14, formed a fine attacking partnership with Tim Coleman and had scored 45 goals in 97 League and Cup games when the outbreak of the First World War ended his first-class career.

PEART, JACK One of football's greatest travellers, Jack Peart enjoyed a career which spanned 19 years and every division of the Football League. He was known as the 'most injured man in football' – a broken leg in 1919 kept him out of the game for two years. His playing career began with his home-town club of South Shields in 1905 and ended in 1924 when he was player-manager of Rochdale. In between he played for Sheffield United, Stoke, Newcastle United, Notts County (where his 28 goals helped them win the Second Division Championship), Birmingham and Derby. After a spell as player-manager of Ebbw Vale, he joined Port Vale and later Norwich before signing for Rochdale. In 1930 he was appointed manager of Bradford City but, after five years, he had not brought any great success to Valley Parade and left to take charge at Fulham. He brought stability to the Craven Cottage club and guided them through the difficult years of the Second World War. In his first season at the helm, Peart led the Cottagers to the FA Cup semi-finals where they lost 2–1 to Sheffield United. In September 1948, after a brief illness, Peart died. Ironically, the Fulham side that he had built went on to win that season's Second Division Championship.

PENN, FRANK One of the club's longest-serving players, Frank Penn joined Fulham in 1915 and made 73 wartime appearances for the Cottagers. His performances in those matches led to him being selected for an England trial for the Victory International matches of 1919. He made his League début in the 1–0 win over South Shields on the opening day of the 1919–20 season, going on to be a first-team regular for the next twelve seasons. The speedy winger, who was noted for his pin-point crosses, laid on numerous goalscoring opportunities for the likes of Donald Cock, Bill Prouse, Sid Elliott and Jimmy Temple, though in 1928–29 he himself netted ten League goals as Fulham finished fifth in the Third Division (South). Penn scored 52 goals all told and played the last of his 460 League and Cup games in March 1934, a 5–1 defeat at West Ham United. Penn qualified as a physiotherapist whilst he was still playing and in 1939 became the Cottagers' first-team trainer, a position he held until his retirement in the summer of 1965.

PERRY, EDDIE Welsh international forward Eddie Perry played his early football for his home-town team Rhymney in the Welsh League. After a number of impressive performances, he was given the chance to play for Merthyr Town and, in an FA Cup tie, almost single-handedly beat Bournemouth. The Cherries were quick to offer him professional terms but he was unable to win a regular place at Dean Court and joined Thames FC. In his first season he was the club's leading scorer with 16 goals, an achievement which prompted Fulham manager James McIntyre to secure his services in the summer of 1931. He made his first-team début for the Cottagers on Christmas Day 1931 when Fulham played out a goalless draw at Brentford. Despite some great goalscoring achievements for the club's reserve side, Perry made just five League appearances in his first three seasons at Craven Cottage. In 1934–35 he was given an extended run in the first-team and scored 15 goals in 19 games including a hat-trick in a 7–0 home win over Notts County. The following season he netted another hat-trick in a 5–1 defeat of Bradford City and scored four goals in a 5–2 FA Cup quarter-final win over Blackpool. He had scored 40 goals in 67 games when he was allowed to leave and join Doncaster Rovers. In 1946 he joined Fulham's coaching staff before being appointed manager of Southend United.

PESCHISOLIDO, PAUL Canadian international Paul Peschisolido began his career with Toronto Blizzards before a £25,000 fee took him to Birmingham City in January 1992. The diminutive striker, who stands just 5ft 4ins, scored 17 goals in 46 League and Cup games before leaving St Andrew's to join Stoke City for £400,000 in the summer of 1994. After two seasons with the Potters in which he scored 22 goals in 75 games, he rejoined Birmingham City (where his wife, Karen Brady, is managing director) on transfer deadline day in March 1996. His return lasted a mere four months and in the summer West Bromwich Albion paid £600,000 for his services. A firm favourite with the Baggies' fans, he had scored 19 goals in 51 games including a hat-trick in a 3–1 win at Bury before becoming Fulham's first £1 million signing in October 1997. He made a goalscoring début in a 1–1 home draw against Northampton Town, going on to score 13 goals in 32 games including a hat-trick in a 5–0 defeat of Carlisle United. He helped the Cottagers win the Second Division Championship in 1998–99, taking his tally of goals to 23 in 75 League and Cup games.

PEYTON, GERRY After unsuccessful trials with Coventry City and West Bromwich Albion and failing to impress Aston Villa, goalkeeper Gerry Peyton joined Southern League club, Atherstone Town. After a number of outstanding displays, he joined Burnley for a fee of £10,000 and kept a clean sheet on his début as the Clarets were held to a goalless draw at Turf Moor by Liverpool. In his early days with Burnley, Peyton shared the goalkeeping duties with Alan Stevenson but it was still a surprise when the Lancashire club allowed him to leave and join Fulham for £35,000 in December 1976. Replacing injured keeper Peter Mellor, Peyton was an immediate success at Craven Cottage, his performances leading to a call-up for the England Under-21 squad. However, Peyton rejected the opportunity in the hope that a chance would come along to represent the Republic of Ireland, the birthplace of his parents. He was not to be disappointed and won the first of 33 caps when he played against Spain in Dublin in February 1977. Peyton was Fulham's first-choice keeper for almost ten years, appearing in 395 League and Cup games before he was given a free transfer and joined Bournemouth in the summer of 1986. He had an outstanding first season at Dean Court as the Cherries stormed to the Third Division Championship and promotion to Division Two for the first time ever. After five seasons on the south coast, he moved to Everton for £80,000 as cover for Neville Southall. Unable to oust the Welsh international, he had loan spells with Bolton, Norwich and Brentford before moving to Japan in a player-coach capacity. He is now in Hong Kong.

PIKE, MARTIN Martin Pike began his career with West Bromwich Albion but could not break into the Baggies' first-team and he left the Hawthorns in the summer of 1983 to join Peterborough United. He had scored nine goals in 149 games for the London Road club when Sheffield United paid £20,000 for his services in August 1986. During his three and a half seasons at Bramhall Lane, Pike helped the Blades rise from the Third to the First Division with successive promotions in 1988–89 and 1989–90 but then injuries and a loss of form cost him his place. Following brief loan spells with Tranmere Rovers and Bolton Wanderers, Pike, who had scored five goals in 151 games for the Yorkshire club, joined Fulham for £65,000 in February 1990. An ever-present in his first season with the club, Pike missed very few games during his time at Craven Cottage where he showed his versatility by playing in a number of different positions. He had scored 15 goals in 205 League and Cup games for the Cottagers when he was allowed to leave on a free transfer to join

Rotherham United in the summer of 1994. The start of his career with the Millmoor club was delayed by an injury picked up in pre-season training and even when he had recovered, he suffered an Achilles tendon problem, which limited his appearances to just nine before being released.

PITCH The Craven Cottage pitch measures 110 yards by 75 yards.

PLASTIC Four Football League clubs have replaced their normal grass playing pitches with artificial surfaces at some stage. Queen's Park Rangers were the first in 1981 but the Loftus Road pitch was discarded in 1988 in favour of a return to turf. Luton Town (1985), Oldham Athletic (1986) and Preston North End (1986) followed. The Cottagers did not play on the Kenilworth Road or Boundary Park plastic and only played once on the Loftus Road surface. That was on 2 March 1983 when Gordon Davies scored Fulham's goal in a 2–1 defeat. Fulham played on Preston North End's Deepdale plastic on five occasions. The first, on 30 April 1988, saw them lose 2–1 with Les Barrett scoring the Cottagers' goal but, in the following season, Fulham won 4–1 with Gordon Davies netting twice. There followed two 1–0 defeats before Fulham won the last meeting on the Deepdale plastic – on 8 February 1992 – 2–1, with former North End favourite Gary Brazil scoring one of Fulham's goals.

PLAY-OFFS Fulham have been involved in divisional play-offs on two occasions, both for promotion, both unsuccessfully. In 1988–89 the Cottagers finished fourth in Division Three and, after a seven-match run without defeat, ensured a play-off position against fifth-placed Bristol Rovers. The Cottagers hadn't scored against the Twerton Park club in either League game (home 0–2 and away 0–0) nor could they score in the two play-off games, losing 1–0 at Twerton Park and 4–0 at Craven Cottage. In 1997–98, Fulham finished sixth in Division Two, beating Wrexham and Gillingham for the final play-off spot on goals scored after the three clubs and fifth-placed Bristol Rovers had all finished the season on 70 points. Fulham took the lead in the semi-final first leg against Grimsby Town when Peter Beardsley converted a 45th-minute penalty. Unfortunately for the Cottagers, David Smith levelled the scores in the second-half before a Kevin Donovan goal gave the Mariners a 1–0 win at Blundell Park.

POINTS Under the three-points-for-a-win system which was introduced in 1981–82, Fulham's best tally is 101 points gained in 1998–99 when the club won the Second Division Championship. However, the club's best points haul under the old two-points-for-a-win system was the 60 in season 1958–59, when they were runners-up in the Second Division, and in 1970–71 when they were runners-up in Division Three. These would have netted them 87 and 84 respectively under the present system. Fulham's worst points record under either system was the meagre 25 points secured in 1968–69 when the club finished bottom of the Second Division.

POSTPONED The bleak winter of 1962–63, described at the time as the modern ice age, proved to be one of the most chaotic seasons in British soccer history. The worst Saturday for League action in that awful winter was 9 February when only seven Football League fixtures went ahead and the entire Scottish League programme was frozen off. The worst Saturday for the FA Cup was 5 January, the day of the third-round when only three of the 32 ties could be played. The Cottagers didn't play a single game in the month of January and though they eventually played their third-round opponents West Ham United on 4 February, the game ended goalless. It was finally settled on 20 February when, despite Bobby Robson netting for the Cottagers, West Ham won 2-1 with goals from Boyce and Byrne.

PRICE, JOHNNY An England Amateur international with Woking, Price joined Fulham in the summer of 1928 and scored on his début in a 2–2 draw at Gillingham on the opening day of the 1928–29 season. He went on to score 13 goals in 29 League games including a hat-trick in a 6-2 win at Watford. Though he continued to score his fair share of goals, Price was an old-fashioned inside-forward, feeding his wingers or creating chances for the centre-forward. At the end of his first season with the Cottagers, he was selected to tour South Africa with the FA and early the following season played for The Rest in an England trial match. In 1931–32 he helped Fulham win the Third Division (South) Championship but a hip injury which was to reduce his number of appearances over the coming years forced him to miss the last ten games of the season. He went on to score 53 goals in 204 games before leaving to try and resurrect his career with Port Vale. He made just 13 appearances for the Valiants before injury forced his retirement. He later coached both Wimbledon and Yiewsley before returning to Craven Cottage as the club's assistant secretary.

PROMOTION The Cottagers have been promoted on seven occasions. They were first promoted in 1931–32 when, after four seasons of playing in the Third Division (South) following their relegation in 1927–28, Fulham won the Championship. Frank 'Bonzo' Newton established a new club scoring record with 43 goals. After ten seasons in the Second Division, Fulham were promoted to the top-flight after winning the 1948–49 Championship but three seasons after they were back in Division Two. The club's third experience of promotion came in 1958–59 when they finished two points behind champions Sheffield Wednesday to return to the First Division. Following the club's longest spell in the top-flight, the Cottagers suffered successive relegations to find themselves starting the 1969–70 season in Division Three. The following season they returned to the Second Division as runners-up to Preston North End, finishing a point behind the Deepdale club. After nine seasons of Second Division football, Fulham were relegated but again following two seasons in the Third Division they were promoted in third place behind Burnley and Carlisle United. Relegation to the Third Division came in 1985–86 but following reorganisation, Fulham found themselves in the 'new' Second Division. The Cottagers were relegated in 1993–94 but after three seasons in the League's basement, won promotion to the Second Division behind champions Wigan Athletic, who finished ahead of Fulham on goal average. The club last won promotion in 1998–99 when, with a record 101 points, they won the Second Division Championship.

PROUSE, BILL Inside-forward Bill Prouse played his early football for Redditch Town before joining Third Division (North) side Rochdale in 1922. He was soon amongst the goals for the Lancashire club and in 1923–24 topped the Spotland side's goalscoring charts with 14 strikes in 40 games. This prompted Fulham manager Andy Ducat to sign him at the end of that campaign and he made a goalscoring début in a 1–1 draw at Bradford City on the opening day of the 1924–25 season. Prouse topped Fulham's scoring charts that season with 16 goals in 33 games including a hat-trick in the 3–1 home win over Crystal Palace. He continued to find the net with great regularity the following season but midway through the 1926–27 campaign he lost his place to Johnny Tonner who had joined the club from Clapton Orient. Prouse, who had scored 32 goals in 84 League and Cup games, left Craven Cottage to play non-League football for Wellington Town.

Q

QUESTED, LEN Folkestone-born wing-half Len Quested played his early football for his home-town team in the Southern League before joining Fulham as an amateur. After only a handful of wartime games, Quested joined the navy but on his return to Craven Cottage in 1946 he signed professional forms and made his League début in a 1–0 home win over Burnley in May 1947. After that he was one of the mainstays of the Fulham side for the next five seasons and in 1948–49 when the Cottagers won the Second Division Championship, he scored his first League goals for the club in a 2–1 win at West Bromwich Albion. In the club's first season in the top-flight, Quested and Bob Thomas were the only ever-presents as they finished in 17th place. Quested's form had been such that he won an England 'B' cap for the match against Holland but yet in October 1951, after he had scored seven goals in 188 games, he was allowed to join Huddersfield Town in exchange for Jeff Taylor. In his second season at Leeds Road, he helped the Yorkshire club win promotion to the First Division and then in 1953–54 finish third in the top-flight. He had played in 220 League games for Huddersfield when he decided to leave the first-class game and emigrate to Australia.

R

RAPID SCORING When Fulham beat Ipswich Town 10–1 on Boxing Day 1963, Graham Leggatt set up a Cottagers' record for rapid scoring by netting a hat-trick in the space of just three minutes! In fact, the club scored four goals in four and a half minutes as Maurice Cook scored the Cottagers' first goal in the 16th minute with a spectacular effort.

RECEIPTS The club's record receipts are £139,235 for the Second Division game at Craven Cottage against Watford on 2 May 1998. A crowd of 17,114 saw Fulham go down 2–1 with Peter Beardsley netting Fulham's goal.

RELEGATION Fulham have been relegated on seven occasions. The club's first experience of relegation was in 1927–28 when, after 17 seasons of Second Division football following their admittance to the Football League, they finished 21st and dropped into the Third Division (South). The club won two championships before their next experience of relegation – winning the Third Division (South) title in 1931–32 and the Second Division title in 1948–49 – but in 1951–52, after three seasons of top-flight football, they finished bottom of the First Division, a point behind Huddersfield Town who finished 21st. The Cottagers returned to the top-flight in 1958–59 but nine seasons later they again finished bottom of the First Division and experienced their third relegation. After a disastrous 1968–69 season, the club suffered their second successive relegation though they did return to the Second Division two seasons later. The club's fifth experience of relegation came in 1979–80 but again just two seasons were needed for the Cottagers to climb out of the Third Division. In 1985–86, Fulham along with Carlisle United and Middlesbrough were relegated to the Third Division. Following reorganisation, Fulham found themselves playing in the 'new' Second Division but in 1993–94 they suffered their seventh and final experience of relegation when Exeter City, Hartlepool United and Barnet joined them in the League's basement.

REYNOLDS, ARTHUR Playing in more games than any other Fulham goalkeeper, Arthur Reynolds began his career with his home-town team, Dartford. He joined the Craven Cottage club in March 1910 and made his début the following month in a 2–2 draw at Lincoln City. After that, Reynolds was the club's first-choice keeper for eleven seasons, making 100 consecutive League and Cup appearances from his début and being ever-present in season's 1910–11, 1911–12, 1921–22 and 1922–23. During the latter two seasons, Reynolds appeared in 118 consecutive League games. Despite being the most outstanding keeper outside the top-flight, Reynolds' only representative honour came in October 1914 when he played for the Football League against the Southern League. Not surprisingly, Reynolds was the subject of enquiries from a number of top clubs, especially League Champions Blackburn Rovers who pursued the matter on a number of occasions. Reynolds, who appeared in 42 games for Fulham during the First World War, had made 420 League and Cup appearances for the Cottagers when he left to join Orient in the summer of 1925. Unable to break into the Brisbane Road club's first-team, the 36-year-old keeper decided to retire.

RICHARDS, BILL Welsh international winger Bill Richards began his League career with Wolverhampton Wanderers, joining the Molineux club with his brother in 1927. After two seasons in which he made 30 appearances, he left to play for Coventry City but when the Highfield Road club were relegated to the Third Division (South) his former manager James McIntyre brought him to Craven Cottage. Richards made his Fulham début against his former club on the opening day of the 1931–32 season, helping the Cottagers beat Coventry 5–3. Fulham went on to win the Third Division (South) Championship that season, with Richards scoring eight goals in 33 games including a hat-trick in the 8–0 rout of Thames. Midway through the following season, Richards won his only cap when he played against Northern Ireland at Wrexham. However, following the signing of Johnny Arnold, his first-team opportunities became rather limited and after scoring 15 goals in 82 games he left to play for Brighton and Hove Albion before ending his career with Bristol Rovers.

ROBSON, BOBBY One of the game's most successful managers, Bobby Robson began his career as an amateur with Middlesbrough but was playing for another local side, Langley Park Juniors, when Fulham manager Bill Dodgin secured his services for the Craven Cottage club in May 1950. He made his League début for Fulham in a 2–2 draw at Sheffield Wednesday towards the end of the 1950–51 season after which he missed very few games, being ever-present in 1954–55. Forming a good understanding with Bedford Jezzard and Johnny Haynes, Robson's performances attracted a number of top-flight clubs and in March 1956 West Bromwich Albion manager Vic Buckingham paid £25,000 to take him to the Hawthorns. During his seven seasons with Albion, Robson was converted from inside-forward to wing-half but it didn't stop him from scoring 61 goals in 240 League games for the Baggies. In 1958, Robson renewed his partnership with Johnny Haynes when he won the first of 20 full caps for England against France. Robson, like Haynes, lost his place in the international side after the 1962 World Cup finals but then linked up with him again when he rejoined the Cottagers for a second spell in the summer of 1962. An ever-present in 1964–65, Robson took his tally of goals for Fulham to 80 in 370 League and Cup games before leaving to manage Vancouver Royals. Within six months he was back at Craven Cottage as manager but lasted less than a year, being sacked for failing to arrest the club's decline. After a short spell scouting for Chelsea, he was appointed manager of Ipswich Town in January 1969. Gradually he began to put together a useful side. The Portman Road club finished fourth in the First Division in both the 1972–73 and 1973–74 seasons. They also finished third in season's 1974–75, 1976–77 and 1979–80 and were runners-up in 1980–81 and 1981–82. The club won the UEFA Cup in 1980 but Robson's greatest triumph came in the 1978 FA Cup final when Ipswich beat Arsenal 1–0. In July 1982, Robson replaced Ron Greenwood as England manager. Although they failed to qualify for the European Championships in 1984 they qualified for the World Cup finals two years later but lost to Argentina in the quarter-finals. In 1990 he took England to the World Cup semi-finals where they were unfortunate to lose to West Germany on

Bobby Robson

penalties after a 1–1 draw. In August 1990 he took over at PSV Eindhoven. They won the Dutch title in both 1990–91 and 1991–92 but failed to find any success in Europe. Robson later managed Sporting Lisbon and Barcelona before replacing Ruud Gullit as manager of Newcastle United.

ROOKE, RONNIE One of the game's most prolific goalscorers, Ronnie Rooke began his career with Crystal Palace during the 1932–33 season. He scored over 150 goals for their reserve side but only made 18 appearances in which he scored four goals for the first-team before joining Fulham in November 1936. He made an immediate impact, scoring a hat-trick for the Cottagers on his début in a 5–0 win over West Ham United. He went on to net three further hat-tricks that season – Southampton (away 3–3) Sheffield United (home 4–0) and Aston Villa (home 3–2) – to finish as the club's leading scorer with 19 goals in 22 games. In fact, Rooke topped the club's scoring charts in all of his eleven seasons with the Cottagers seven of which were during the Second World War. In 1937–38 his total of 17 goals in 27 games included four in the 8–1 rout of Swansea Town and hat-tricks against Blackburn Rovers (home 3–1) and Bury (home 4–0). In 1938–39 he scored four goals in a 5–3 win at Manchester City and netted all six in a 6–0 FA Cup win at Bury, ending the season with 26 goals in 40 games. During the Second World War, Ronnie Rooke scored 212 goals in just 199 games and played for England against Wales in a wartime international in October 1942. When League football resumed in 1946–47, Rooke had scored 13 goals in 18 games when he was transferred to Arsenal for £1,000 with David Nelson and Cyril Grant joining the Cottagers in part-exchange. Rooke had scored 77 goals in 110 League and Cup games for Fulham. At the age of 35, Ronnie Rooke found himself playing top-flight football for the first time and on his début at Charlton Athletic, scored the winning goal. He went on to score 21 goals in 24 games and save the Gunners from relegation whilst in 1947–48 he scored 30, still a post-war Arsenal goalscoring record. He finished that season as the First Division's leading goalscorer and helped Arsenal win the League Championship. He went on to score 70 goals in 94 games before rejoining Crystal Palace as player-manager in June 1949. He scored 26 goals in 46 games for the Selhurst Park club before ending his involvement with the game after a spell as manager of non-League Bedford.

ROSS, HARRY Brechin-born defender Harry Ross began his career with his home-town club before moving south of the border to play for First Division Burnley. In three seasons with the Turf Moor club, Ross appeared in 105 League games before leaving the Clarets to join Fulham in the summer of 1904. He made his début for the Cottagers in a 1–0 win at Tottenham Hotspur on the opening day of the 1904–05 season, going on to appear in 99 Southern League games and winning two Championship medals. In the club's last season in the Southern League, Ross was selected to play in a Scottish international trial and was unlucky not to win full honours. He made his Football League début in the 1–0 defeat at home to Hull City, the club's first game in the competition but after 29 games, the last being a 3–2 home defeat by Glossop on the opening day of the 1908–09 season, he was transferred to St Mirren where he ended his first-class career.

ROWLEY, ARTHUR Arthur Rowley became the most prolific scorer in the Football League, yet, though he gave early promise of feats to come, his home-town club Wolverhampton Wanderers failed to sign him on professional forms. He made his senior début, as an amateur, alongside his brother Jack, just five days after his 15th birthday, in a wartime Manchester United fixture at Anfield. He signed professional forms for West Bromwich Albion and made his League début for them in 1946. On December 1948 he joined Fulham in exchange for Ernie Shepherd and made his début in a 3–1 home win over Grimsby Town. He scored 19 goals in 22 games that season, a total which included four in the 7–2 win over Bury and a hat-trick in the following match as Plymouth Argyle were beaten 6–1. He went on to score 26 goals in 59 games for the Cottagers before moving to Leicester City in the summer of 1950 for £12,000. In eight seasons at Filbert Street, Rowley, who gained England 'B' and Football League honours, established goalscoring records for the Foxes that would never be broken. He scored 251 goals in 303 League games with a best of 44 in the club's Second Division Championship-winning season of 1956–57. He was transferred to Shrewsbury Town in June 1958 where he continued to find the net, taking his tally of League goals to 434 from 619 games. He later managed the Gay Meadow club before taking charge at Sheffield United, Southend United and Oswestry Town.

RUSSELL, HARRY Enlisted with the Lancashire Fusiliers, Harry Russell served in India, where he learned to play hockey and represented both the Army and his country. He lived in India for five years and on his return to England he walked into the office at Craven Cottage and asked for a trial. Fulham liked what they saw, signed the Gravesend-born defender, and he played his début in March 1913, a 3–2 win over Birmingham. In the two seasons leading up to the outbreak of the First World War, Russell formed an outstanding half-back line with Alf Marshall and Jimmy Torrance although he also appeared at full-back and wing-half as well as his preferred position of centre-half. He was still the club's first-choice pivot when League football resumed in

1919–20 but subsequent injuries and a loss of form limited his appearances. He had scored seven goals in 143 League and Cup games when in 1925 he left to play non-League football for Sheppey United.

S

SCOTT, PETER Midfielder Peter Scott had just had a trial with Manchester United when Fulham stepped in and signed him on apprentice forms in May 1980. Within a month of signing professional forms in September 1981, Scott had made his League début in a 1–0 defeat at Huddersfield Town. That was his only first-team appearance, apart from one as a substitute in a League Cup tie at Coventry City, until 1983–84 when he won a regular place in the side. He remained an important member of the Fulham side for the next nine seasons and had scored 34 goals in 306 League and Cup games when, in August 1992, he was allowed to join Bournemouth on a free transfer. After just one season with the Cherries, he moved to Barnet where he was made club captain. He went on to score three goals in 96 League and Cup games for the Bees before being released in the summer of 1996.

SECOND DIVISION Fulham have had eight spells in the Second Division, beginning in 1907–08 following their admission to the Football League. This first spell, the club's longest in the Second Division, lasted for 17 seasons until they were relegated in 1927–28. The club returned to Division Two for a second spell in 1931–32 and came close to winning the Championship in their first season back but finished third, six points behind champions Stoke. The Cottagers did eventually win the Second Division Championship in 1948–49 but after just three seasons of top-flight football, returned to Division Two for a third spell. The club won promotion after seven seasons and there followed nine seasons of top-flight football before the club returned to the Second Division for the 1968–69 season. A disastrous campaign, they finished bottom, which led to a second successive relegation. They rejoined Division Two in 1970–71. After nine seasons the club were relegated to the Third Division, again winning promotion after two seasons. The club's sixth spell in Division Two began with the Cottagers coming close to winning promotion but eventually they had to settle for fourth place. After two seasons of mid-table placings, Fulham were relegated in 1985–86 but in 1992–93, following reorganisation, found themselves in the 'new' Second Division. Relegated in 1993–94, the Cottagers bounced back two seasons later to begin their eighth and final spell in the Second Division, culminating in their winning the Championship in 1998–99.

SEMI-FINALS The Cottagers have been involved in five FA Cup semi-finals and one in the Anglo-Scottish Cup competition.

SHARP, JIMMY Left-back Jimmy Sharp began his career with Dundee during the 1899–1900 season. He spent five seasons at Dens Park, helping the club to the Scottish Championship runners-up position in 1902–03 and winning the first of five Scottish caps against Wales in 1904. Sharp joined Fulham in readiness for the 1904–05 season and made his début in a 1–0 win at Tottenham Hotspur on the opening day of that campaign. At the end of the season, Sharp left Craven Cottage to join Woolwich Arsenal. The sturdy little defender made 116 appearances for the Gunners before being transferred to Glasgow Rangers in April 1908 for £400. His stay at Ibrox Park lasted just nine months before Fulham manager Phil Kelso paid £1,000 to take him back to Craven Cottage. Sharp became an important member of the Fulham side, missing very few games until November 1912, when he left to try his luck in the United States. Within months he had returned to England and joined Chelsea. He enjoyed three seasons at Stamford Bridge till the outbreak of the First World War. He officially retired during the hostilities and in 1919 returned to Craven Cottage as Fulham's trainer. However, when Fulham's inside-left Harold Crockford missed the club's bus to an away game at Bury in 1920, Sharp at the age of almost 40 not only filled in but scored his one and only goal for the Cottagers in a 2–2 draw. He later coached at both Walsall and Cliftonville.

SHEA, DANNY A superb ball-player and a consistent goalscorer, Danny Shea began his career playing in the Southern League for West Ham United. After replacing the long-serving Billy Grassam, he became the club's leading goalscorer for five seasons from 1908 to 1913. During the 1908–09 season he scored all four goals in a 4–0 defeat of Plymouth Argyle and a hat-trick in a 4–2 win over Swindon Town. His most prolific season for the Hammers was 1909–10 when he netted 31 in 43 League and Cup games. He netted another four goals in December 1910 as West Ham won 6–0 at Southend United and, not surprisingly, won Southern League representative honours. He had scored 110 goals in 169 games for the Hammers when, midway through the 1912–13 season, he left to join Blackburn Rovers. The Ewood Park club broke the existing transfer record to take Shea to Lancashire where he continued to score on a regular basis. With Blackburn, Shea won three England caps and Football League representative honours as well as scoring 27 goals in Rovers' Championship-winning season of 1913–14. During the war years he returned south and in 73 wartime games, as a 'guest' for West Ham, scored 63 goals. He also 'guested' for Fulham, Birmingham and Nottingham Forest before spending one more season with Blackburn Rovers. He left Ewood Park in the summer of 1920 to rejoin the Hammers but, after just 16 appearances, he moved to Fulham. Shea made his Fulham début in a 3–0 defeat at Clapton Orient but soon began to demonstrate that he still had plenty of football left in him. He was an important member of the Fulham side for three seasons, scoring 24 goals in 107 games including a hat-trick in the 3–0 home win over Stockport County in March 1923. On leaving Craven Cottage, Shea played for Coventry City, Clapton Orient and Sheppey United before later working in the docks of London's East End.

SHERPA VAN TROPHY The competition for Associate Members of the Football League was first sponsored by Sherpa Van in the 1987–88 season. Fulham's first match in the Sherpa Van Trophy saw them lose 1–0 at Southend United before they were beaten 6–1 at Craven Cottage by Brighton and Hove Albion. In 1988–89 Fulham again lost both group games against Brentford (home 0–2) and Gillingham (away 1–2) and thus, in two years in the competition, failed to win a single game.

SKENE, LESLIE It was whilst studying to be a doctor at Edinburgh University that Leslie Skene first showed an interest in goalkeeping. He began his career with Stenhousemuir but he left to play for Queen's Park after just one season. He spent six seasons with the Hampden Park club during which time he was capped by Scotland at full international level against Wales in 1904. Skene left Queen's Park in the summer of 1907 to join Fulham, making his début in the 1–0 home defeat by Hull City in the club's first-ever Football League game. He went on to give some outstanding displays as the Cottagers finished fourth in Division Two and reached the FA Cup semi-finals. He was the club's first choice keeper for three seasons, appearing in 94 games before leaving in 1910 to play for Glentoran. During his time at The Oval, the Larbert-born goalkeeper represented the Irish League, eventually leaving the game to work in a mental hospital in the Isle of Man just before the outbreak of the First World War.

SKINNER, JUSTIN Hounslow-born midfielder Justin Skinner made his League début for Fulham in February 1987 in a 1–1 home draw against Rotherham United. He won a regular place in the Cottagers' side in 1987–88, playing in 38 games and scoring seven goals. That season saw him voted Young Player of the Year by the Fulham supporters. Maturing into an accomplished midfield player, he not only had delightful control and good distribution of the ball, but notched up an impressive record from the penalty spot. He had scored 27 goals in 152 League and Cup games when in the summer of 1991 he left Craven Cottage to join Bristol Rovers for their then club record fee of £130,000. He soon became an influential member of the Rovers' side, his accurate free kicks and corners being an important source of the club's goal-scoring opportunities. Sadly, he broke his leg in an Auto Windscreen Shield tie against Fulham, but recovered and regained his place in the Twerton Park club's side. Following a loan spell with Walsall, Skinner, who had scored 12 goals in 207 games for Bristol Rovers, left to play Scottish League football for Hibernian.

SLOUGH, ALAN Utility player Alan Slough began his career with his home-town club Luton Town and in eight seasons with the Kenilworth Road club scored 28 goals in 275 games, winning a Fourth Division Championship medal in 1967–68. He left the Hatters in the summer of 1973, joining Fulham for a fee of £45,000. He made his début in a 2–0 home win over Millwall on the opening day of the 1973–74 season and, over the next four seasons, missed very few games, being ever-present in 1976–77. He was also an important member of the Cottagers side that reached Wembley in 1975 and captained the club in his last season at Craven Cottage following Alan Mullery's retirement.

Alan Slough

Slough had scored 17 goals in 187 League and Cup games when, in July 1977, he was allowed to join Peterborough United for £25,000. He spent four seasons at London Road as player-coach, scoring ten goals in 105 League appearances, including a hat-trick of penalties against Chester. He joined Millwall in a similar capacity before coaching Torquay United. He later moved into non-League football, first with Weymouth and then Yeovil and Minehead and is currently player-manager of Torquay Christians in the South Devon League.

SMALLEST PLAYER Although such statistics are always unreliable for those playing in the early part of the last century, it appears that the distinction of being Fulham's smallest player goes to Pat Flanagan who was known as 'Little Jack'. Standing around 5ft 3ins, the scheming inside-forward played regularly for Norwich City and Arsenal but made only 11 appearances for the Cottagers. The club's current Canadian international Paul Peschisolido is 5ft 4ins tall.

SMITH, JAMES Preston-born winger James Smith began his Football League career with Bury in 1903 but in three seasons with the Shakers he made just 21 appearances before being released. He drifted into non-League football first with Stalybridge Celtic and then Accrington Stanley before joining Chorley at the start of the 1908–09 season. His goalscoring exploits at Victory Park prompted Fulham manager Harry Bradshaw to bring him to Craven Cottage. A speedy winger whose pin-point crosses provided a number of goalscoring opportunities for his team-mates, he made his Fulham début in a 2–1 home defeat by Clapton Orient. Though not a great goalscorer, he ended the 1910–11 season, in which Fulham finished tenth in Division Two, as the club's leading scorer with 11 goals. He continued to be the Cottagers' first-choice right-winger up until the outbreak of the First World War when he had taken his tally of goals to 19 in 194 League and Cup outings.

SMITH, TREVOR After beginning his career with South Moors in his native Durham, Trevor Smith became a semi-professional with Anfield Plain in 1930. After a series of impressive performances, Charlton Athletic signed him on professional forms but he couldn't settle at The Valley and in March 1935 he joined Fulham for a fee of £1,000. Smith made his début for the Cottagers in a 2–1 home win over Bolton Wanderers and went on to play in five of the remaining nine games. Midway through the following season he switched from outside-right to inside-right to accommodate Fulham's new signing, Bert Worsley, from Leeds United. Smith revelled in his new position and was instrumental in the Cottagers reaching that season's FA Cup semi-final. He had scored 21 goals in 100 games for Fulham when in January 1938 he was transferred to Crystal Palace for £2,500. During the Second World War, Smith 'guested' for Fulham but when the war ended he had brief spells with Yeovil Town and Colchester United before returning to League action with Watford.

SONG During the club's run to the FA Cup final in 1975, the Fulham supporters sang the words below to the tune of 'Y Viva España':

Oh this year we're going to win the Cup,
Hey viva El Fulham,
Then next year, you know we're going up,
Hey viva El Fulham.
Alan M is a wonder, that's for sure,
Hey viva El Fulham,
And Bobby – well do we need say Moore?
It's Fulham por favor.

SOUTHERN LEAGUE Fulham's first season in the Southern League, 1898–99, proved to be a disruptive one. After a poor start, the club embraced professionalism in December 1898, a decision that upset a number of the long-serving players who decided to leave the club in protest. This crisis led to a large turnover of players and in just 22 games, 41 players were used. Fulham finished tenth in their first season in the Southern League Second Division. In 1899–1900, Fulham finished in second place, six points behind champions Watford, but then lost to Thames Ironworks in the Test Matches, as the play-offs were called at the time. Fulham must have felt aggrieved when Queen's Park Rangers were elected straight into Division One of the Southern League, whilst they still languished in Division Two. The following season the Cottagers finished fifth, having had to play two fixtures on the same day. The first-team won 3–0 at home to Sheppey United whilst the reserves went to Wycombe Wanderers and were losing 3–0 at half-time when the game was abandoned. In 1901–02 Fulham were the Second Division champions, pipping Grays United by a point. Unfortunately they lost their Test Match to Swindon Town 3–1 at Reading and were not promoted, even though the Wiltshire club had gained only seven points from 30 games. There were so few fixtures in the Second Division of the Southern League that the Cottagers had to rejoin the London League. Fulham regained their Second Division title in 1902–03, winning all five home games without conceding a goal. Despite losing the Test Match 7–2 to Brentford, the club were advised that, if they could raise a first-class team by the end of May 1903, they would be admitted to the First Division of the Southern League. Playing in the Southern League First Division for the first time in 1903–04, Fulham finished 11th. They moved up to sixth in 1904–05 and in doing so recorded their best-ever victory in the Southern League when they beat Wellingborough 12–0, with Fraser scoring five and Wardrope a hat-trick. Prior to the start of the 1905–06 season, Fulham made a number of new signings and, in the run up to Christmas, lost only one game. Southampton were the only side to stay with the Cottagers but the London side won their last four games to clinch the title by five points. Fulham gained the title for the second year in succession in 1906–07 when their nearest rivals were Portsmouth. The Fratton Park club led the table at the turn of the year but when the two sides met at Craven Cottage in February 1907, it was Fulham who triumphed 2–0. They then embarked on a run of 11 games without defeat, clinching the title after a 3–0 win over Southampton in the penultimate game of the season. The club then applied to join the Football League and, after polling 25 votes, equal highest with Lincoln, were duly elected.

SPONSORS The club's present sponsors are Demon Internet. Previous sponsors have included GMB and Teleconnect.

STANNARD, JIM Goalkeeper Jim Stannard joined the Cottagers from Ford United and made his début for them in a 2–0 home win over Swindon Town in January 1981 when a goalkeeping crisis forced the club to blood the youngster. He held his place to the end of the season, keeping six clean sheets in 17 games. He returned to the club's reserve side for the next two seasons as Gerry Peyton returned to help the club win promotion to the Second Division as champions of Division Three. Stannard had loan spells with Southend United and Charlton Athletic before leaving to join the Shrimpers on a permanent basis in March 1985. He played well for the Roots Hall club and in his second season there helped Southend win promotion to the Third Division. He had appeared in 118 first-team games when Fulham paid £50,000 to bring him back to Craven Cottage. Stannard was the club's first-choice keeper for the next eight seasons, going on to play in 428 League and Cup games in his two spells with the Cottagers – the highest by a Fulham keeper. The brave, acrobatic goalkeeper was the club's longest-serving professional when he left Craven Cottage in the summer of 1995 to play for Gillingham. In his first season at the Priestfield Stadium, he was voted the club's Player of the Year and elected to the PFA divisional team. Injuries restricted his appearances but whenever he was called upon, he never let the side down and appeared in 126 games before joining the club's coaching staff.

STAPLETON, JOE It was whilst doing his National Service with the RASC in Egypt that wing-half Joe Stapleton signed for Southall FC. Yet when he returned home, he joined Hayes before moving to Uxbridge and helped them win the Corinthian Memorial Shield. His performances attracted a lot of attention from a number of League clubs. Fulham manager Bill Dodgin senior secured Stapleton's services in the summer of 1952 but, despite impressing in the Cottagers' reserve side, he had to wait until April 1955 before making his League début in a 5–1 home win over Swansea Town. Also able to play centre-half, Stapleton was an important member of the Fulham side for four seasons, scoring two goals in 104 appearances before a serious ankle injury ended his first-class career. However, after a short spell out of the game, he returned to action with non-League Cambridge City in 1961.

STEELE, ALEX Utility player Alex Steele was playing Irish League football for Glenavon when Charlton Athletic, who had just been admitted to the Football League, secured his services. He spent five seasons at The Valley, making 146 first-team appearances before leaving to play for Swansea Town in the summer of 1926. However, when Swans' manager Joe Bradshaw left to take over the reins at Craven Cottage, Steele followed him, joining the Cottagers for a fee of £500. The Northern Ireland international made his début in a 2–2 home draw against Preston North End on the opening day of the season and, though he suffered from injuries during his three seasons with the club, he still managed to appear in 54 League and Cup games for the Cottagers. At the end of the 1929–30 season, Steele retired and returned to his native Ireland to run a newsagent's shop on the outskirts of Belfast. However, he still maintained his connections with the game, acting as a scout for Blackpool for a good number of years.

STEVENS, ARTHUR Goalscoring winger Arthur Stevens played his early football in the Isthmian League with Wimbledon before joining the ground-staff of Brentford. On the outbreak of the Second World War, Stevens was forced to leave Griffin Park and went to play for Sutton until 1941 when he joined Fulham. He appeared in a handful of wartime games for the Cottagers but most of his time was spent fighting overseas. When League football resumed in 1946–47, Stevens won a regular place in the Fulham side, kept his position for twelve seasons and was ever-present in 1948–49 and 1950–51. He netted the first of his three hat-tricks for the club in an FA Cup fourth-round tie against Bristol Rovers in January 1948 as Fulham ran out winners 5–2. When the Cottagers won the Second Division Championship in 1948–49, Stevens, who scored 12 goals, netted his first League hat-trick in a 5–0 home win over Queen's Park Rangers. His best season was 1956–57 when his total of 17 included his final hat-trick for the club in a 3–1 home defeat of Grimsby Town. The following season he helped Fulham reach the FA Cup semi-finals where they lost to Manchester United after a replay. During that Cup run, Stevens scored five goals including strikes in each of the two matches against the Old Trafford club. In fact, his record of 14 goals in 27 FA Cup ties is one of the best in the club's history. Stevens had scored 124 goals in 413 League and Cup games when he lost his place in the side to Graham Leggatt. However, he remained at Craven Cottage, working on the coaching staff until the appointment of Vic Buckingham as manager in 1965.

STOCK, ALEC Alec Stock was on the books of both Tottenham Hotspur and Charlton Athletic before making his League début for Queen's Park Rangers against Reading in February 1938. He made a handful of appearances before war was declared, and also 'guested' for a number of clubs before joining the Royal Armoured Corps, eventually reaching the rank of major. At the age of 26, Stock became player-manager of Yeovil Town and their famous FA Cup victory over Sunderland pushed him into the limelight. In August 1949 he became manager of Leyton Orient, guiding them to some enjoyable Cup runs and into Division Two before spending a 53–day stint as Arsenal's assistant manager. After returning to Brisbane Road, Stock spent three months as manager of AS Roma before another spell at Orient, whom he finally left in February 1959. He was appointed manager of Queen's Park Rangers in August that year and soon began to rebuild the side. In 1967 Stock achieved for Rangers a unique double of the Third Division Championship and Wembley victory in the League Cup final. The following season, Rangers won promotion to Division One, but, with internal pressures mounting, Stock resigned. Appointed manager of Luton Town in December 1968, he led the Hatters to promotion from Division Three but, in the summer of 1972, he moved to Craven Cottage to take charge of Fulham. Stock soon entered the transfer market, bringing players like Alan Mullery, Bobby Moore and George Best to Craven Cottage. His greatest triumph was to take the Cottagers to the FA Cup final of 1975. However, financial problems at the club, coupled with the ousting of the old board of directors, led to his departure in December 1976. One of football's true gentlemen, he became a director at Queen's Park Rangers in April 1977, was caretaker manager at Loftus Road in July 1978 after the departure of Frank Sibley and then manager of Bournemouth for a year before being appointed to the board. He left Dean Court in 1986 but still took an interest in the game through his local club, Swanage Town and Herston.

STRONG, LES Though he was on Crystal Palace's books as a schoolboy, Les Strong joined Fulham as an apprentice in February 1970, turning professional in the summer of 1971. After a season in the club's reserve side, he made his League début as a winger in a 1–1 home draw against Orient in September 1972. He went on to appear in 20 League games, scoring two goals in that position that season but reverted to full-back in 1973. After that, Strong missed very few games over the next eight seasons, being ever-present in 1976–77 and 1981–82 when he skippered the club to promotion to the Second Division. In fact, during that six-season spell, the ever-dependable Strong missed just four League games. In 1974–75, Strong played in all eleven FA Cup ties before the final and was looking forward to playing against West Ham United at Wembley when injury robbed him of the chance. Later the FA struck a special medal for him as compensation. He went on to score six goals in 427 League and Cup games before joining Crystal Palace, following a brief loan spell with Brentford. He stayed for one season at Selhurst Park, making just seven League appearances for the Eagles before playing one game for Rochdale prior to hanging up his boots.

SUART, BOB Stockport-born wing-half Bob Suart played his early football with his home-town club but made only six appearances in his first season, one which saw County fail to gain re-election to the Second Division. When the Edgeley Park club returned to the Lancashire Combination, Suart took the opportunity of establishing himself as a first-team regular in the Stockport side. On County's return to the Football League, Suart continued to impress and after appearing in 119 games he left to join Fulham in a double deal along with Bob Carter for a fee of £500 in March 1908. Suart made his début for the Cottagers against Wolves the following month, scoring the club's opening goal in a 4–1 win. A regular in the Fulham side for the next three seasons, he won a London Challenge Cup winners' medal in 1909–10 when the Cottagers beat Spurs in the final. He went on to appear in 102 League and Cup games for Fulham before joining Burslem Port

Vale, who were then a non-League club, in 1911. He appeared for Stockport in 22 wartime fixtures before being killed in the latter stages of the First World War.

SUBSTITUTES The first-ever Fulham substitute was Graham Leggatt who came on for Johnny Haynes in the 3–0 home defeat by Chelsea on 28 August 1965. The club had to wait until 28 March 1967 for their first goalscoring substitute when Steve Earle scored in the 2–1 defeat at Manchester United. The greatest number of substitutes used in a single season by the Cottagers under the single substitute rule was 34 in 1980–81. From 1986–87, two substitutes were allowed and in 1990–91 the club used 63. From 1996–97, a new rule allowed three substitutes; in that first season, 99 were used and Paul Brooker established a new club record that season when he appeared as a substitute in 26 League matches. He also holds the club record for the most substitute appearances in a career with 43 in the League since his début in October 1995.

SUNDAY FOOTBALL The first-ever Sunday matches in the Football League took place on 20 January 1974 during the three-day week imposed by the Government during the trial of strength with the coalminers. Fulham travelled to Millwall and lost 1–0 at The Den in front of a 15,134 crowd.

SUSTAINED SCORING During the 1931–32 season, Frank Newton scored 43 goals in 39 games to set a League scoring record for the Cottagers. He scored two on the opening day of the season in a 5–3 home win over Coventry City and a hat-trick at Exeter City four days later. He scored in eight of the first nine games of the season and netted further hat-tricks in the matches against Coventry City (away 5–5) and Luton Town (away 3–1).

SYMONS, KIT A highly rated central defender, Symons joined Portsmouth straight from school and soon became captain of the youth side before being given his League début by Alan Ball in a 2–1 defeat at Leicester City in January 1989. Over the next few seasons, he made only a handful of appearances but he was ever-present in 1991–92 and scored his first League goal in a 2–0 win over Burnley on the final day of the season. Symons went on to win Welsh international honours and captain his club before former boss Alan Ball, then in charge of Manchester City, took him to Maine Road for a fee of £1.6 million. Symons, who had scored 11 goals in 204 games for Pompey, proved to be an excellent buy for City where he formed a formidable central defensive partnership with Keith Curle. He missed very few games for the Maine Road club in his first two seasons and was made captain but injuries and a loss of form cost him his place and after playing in 139 games, he joined Fulham on a free transfer in the summer of 1998. The Welsh international, who has won 31 caps, made his Fulham début in a 1–0 win at Macclesfield on the opening day of the season, going on to miss just one game as the Cottagers won the Second Division Championship. His outstanding form at the heart of the Fulham defence was the major reason that the club only conceded 32 goals. Symons, who scored 11 goals in that campaign, is one of the players whose experience, the fans hope, will take them up into the Premiership

T

TALLEST PLAYER It is impossible to be sure who has been the tallest player on Fulham's books as such records are notoriously unreliable. One player likely to lay claim to the title is Shaun Gore at 6ft 4 ins. He made 26 League appearances for the Cottagers before leaving to play for Halifax Town.

TAYLOR, JIM The club's first England international, centre-half Jim Taylor joined the Cottagers as an inside-forward from Hillingdon British Legion club in March 1938. As with many other players of his generation, the Second World War delayed his introduction to League football though he did appear in 88 wartime games for the club. Taylor was 28 years old when he made his League début for Fulham in a 7–2 defeat at Bury on the opening day of the 1946–47 season, a campaign in which he went on to be ever-present. Taylor in fact missed very few games over the next seven seasons, helping the Cottagers win the Second Division Championship in 1948–49. He had represented the Football League in March 1948 and toured Canada with the FA in 1950 before winning his England caps against Argentina and Portugal in the Festival of Britain matches in 1951. Taylor went on to score five goals in 278 League and Cup games before leaving Craven Cottage in the summer of 1953 to play for Queen's Park Rangers. After just one season at Loftus Road, when he appeared in 41 League games, he left to become player-manager of Tunbridge Wells. He later ended his involvement with the game following a spell as manager of Yiewsley Town.

TEMPLE, JIMMY Jimmy Temple, whose uncle George had played for Hull City for seven seasons prior to the outbreak of the First World War, joined Fulham in 1926. After making his début in a 5–0 defeat at Darlington, Temple went on to score two goals in 18 games as Fulham finished 18th in the Second Division. The club continued to struggle in 1927–28 and were relegated to the Third Division (South). However, in 1928–29 Temple had an outstanding season, netting 26 goals in 42 games to top the club's scoring charts. He continued to find the net the following season, scoring his only hat-trick for the Cottagers in a 4–2 win at Torquay United. He had scored 61 goals in 168 League and Cup games when Sunderland took him to Roker Park in part-exchange for Albert Wood and an undisclosed fee. Unable to command a regular place in the Wearsiders' team, Temple left to end his career with Gateshead. The Scarborough-born winger was killed on active service during the Second World War.

TEST MATCHES Test Matches were the early forerunners of today's promotion and relegation play-offs. After finishing runners-up in the Southern League Second Division in 1899–1900, Fulham found themselves playing Thames Ironworks, in a Test Match at White Hart Lane. Ironworks, who had finished 14th in the First Division, kept their place in the top-flight with a 5–1 win over the Cottagers, thanks to a Bill Joyce hat-trick. In 1901–02 Fulham won the Second Division Championship, beating Grays United by a point. Unfortunately they lost their Test Match to Swindon Town 3–1 at Reading and were not promoted, even though Swindon had gained only seven points from 30 matches in the First Division. The Cottagers won the Second Division Championship again the following season but were well beaten 7–2 by Brentford in the Test Match at Shepherd's Bush. However, the club were finally admitted to the First Division of the Southern League for the following season after managing to raise a first-class side.

THIRD DIVISION The Cottagers have had five spells in the Third Division. Their first, which began in 1928–29 following relegation from Division Two, lasted for four seasons before they won the Championship in 1931–32. Ten seasons of Second Division football, promotion to Division One and successive relegations found Fulham back in the Third Division for the start of the 1969–70 season. Promotion in 1970–71 led to nine seasons in Division Two, but in 1980 Fulham were back in the Third

Division for two seasons before winning promotion. The club's fourth spell in the Third Division, which began in 1986–87, lasted for six seasons before reorganisation saw them start the 1992–93 campaign in the 'new' Second Division. The club's final spell in the Third Division began in 1994–95 and lasted three seasons.

THOMAS, BOB On leaving school, Bob Thomas worked as a copy-boy at the *Daily Express*, playing non-League football for Romford, Hayes and Golders Green before joining Brentford's ground-staff in 1939. During the Second World War he served in the Navy but when the hostilities ended he didn't return to Griffin Park, preferring to join his brother Dave at Plymouth Argyle. Bob Thomas had scored 17 goals in 41 League games for the Pilgrims when Fulham manager Jack Peart paid £4,000 to take him to Craven Cottage in the summer of 1947. Thomas's first game in Fulham colours came on the opening day of the 1947–48 season when he scored one of the goals in a 5–0 win over Brentford. When Fulham won the Second Division Championship in 1948–49, Thomas top-scored with 23 goals in 40 games. Though he found goals harder to come by in the top-flight, he was still the club's leading scorer over the next two seasons, taking his tally to 57 in 176 League and Cup games before leaving to play for Crystal Palace in 1952. He spent three seasons at Selhurst Park, scoring 31 goals in 96 games before moving into non-League football with Tunbridge Wells, who were managed by former Fulham favourite Jim Taylor. On hanging up his boots, Thomas went back to work in Fleet Street.

THOMAS, GLEN Left-back Glen Thomas joined Fulham via the YTS scheme in August 1984, signing professional forms in October 1985. He made his first-team début as a substitute for Wayne Kerrins in the Full Members' Cup at Shrewsbury in October 1986, a match that ended goalless. After that, Thomas, who towards the end of his nine seasons at Craven Cottage showed his versatility by appearing in a number of different positions, missed very few games. The popular Hackney-born player had scored six goals in 295 first-team games when he was allowed to join Peterborough United on a free transfer in November 1994. Unable to settle at London Road, he soon left to play for Barnet, where he was a virtual ever-present until his £30,000 transfer to Gillingham in January 1996. After helping the Kent club to the runners-up spot in the Second Division in his first season at the Priestfield Stadium, he was lucky not to lose his eye when he fell during training and a tree branch nearly blinded him. Released by the club in the summer of 1998, he joined Brighton and Hove Albion but injury forced his retirement from the game.

THOMAS, SID Diminutive winger Sid Thomas played his early football for Welsh League club Treharris before Fulham manager Jack Peart brought him to Craven Cottage in 1938. Though he played in a handful of wartime games for the Cottagers, he had to wait eight years before making his League début for the club – a 1–1 home draw against Tottenham Hotspur – in November 1946. Though he was never a regular in the Fulham side, his performances when he did turn out led to his winning four full international caps for Wales. He had scored four goals in 61 outings when he was transferred to Bristol City for £9,000 in the summer of 1950. Having played just 13 games for the Robins, Thomas was taken seriously ill with tuberculosis and forced to quit the game. After a long dispute between the two clubs over the transfer fee, the Ashton Gate club eventually paid up in full.

THRELFALL, FRED Winger Fred Threlfall began his career with Manchester City where his mentor was the great Welsh international Billy Meredith. He was one of the few City players not involved when the FA uncovered financial irregularities at Hyde Road and slapped fines and suspensions on the majority of players and management, almost causing the club to fold. He had appeared in 74 games for City when, in the summer of 1905, he moved to Fulham. He made his début in a goalless home draw against Portsmouth on the opening day of the 1905–06 season, a campaign in which he was ever-present and Fulham won the Southern League Championship. He won another Championship medal the following season when he also played in the Professionals v Amateurs international trial. He made his Football League début for the Cottagers in the 1–0 defeat at home to Hull City in the club's inaugural game in the competition, also helping the club reach that season's FA Cup semi-finals. He had scored 19 goals in 107 games when he left to play for Leicester Fosse in July 1909. He turned in some scintillating performances during his two seasons with the Foxes, combining his playing role with that as a member of the management committee of the Players Union. He later became trainer to the Irish club Cliftonville.

TIGANA, JEAN Former French international Jean Tigana was appointed Fulham manager with effect from 1 July 2000 after agreeing terms of a £7.5 million five-year deal with the Cottagers' chairman Mohamed Al Fayed in April. Al Fayed, the owner of luxury London department store Harrods, has pumped millions of pounds into the club and is likely to release more funds for Tigana to spend on new players. Tigana won 52 full caps for France, helping them reach the World Cup semi-finals in 1982 and 1986 and win the European Championship in 1984, as well as playing for Toulon, Lyon, Bordeaux and Marseilles in a career that spanned 17 years. During his time with Bordeaux he won three French titles and in 1986–87 helped them complete the 'double'. He won another two French titles with Marseilles before retiring as a player. After a spell as Lyon coach he became manager of Monaco but resigned halfway through the 1998–99 season.

TOMPKINS, JIMMY Left-half Jimmy Tompkins played his early football for Isthmian League club Woking. After a series of outstanding displays, he was offered a place on Arsenal's ground-staff at the same time as Fulham had signed him as an amateur. There followed some lengthy and often heated discussions between Gunners' manager Herbert Chapman and Fulham boss James McIntyre. Eventually, in March 1932, Tompkins became a Fulham player but spent the next eighteen months in the club's reserve side. He made his League début for the Cottagers in a 1–0 home win over Swansea Town in September 1933 but made only five appearances over the next two seasons. It was early in the 1935–36 season that Tompkins made the breakthrough into the Fulham side, helping them to reach that season's FA Cup semi-finals. Tompkins, who was ever-present in 1937–38 and 1938–39, had scored five goals in 163 League and Cup games when his career was interrupted by the outbreak of the Second World War. Jimmy Tompkins, who attained the rank of major, was killed on D-Day.

TOOTILL, ALF Nicknamed 'The Birdcatcher', goalkeeper Alf Tootill began his playing career with Ramsbottom United in the Bury Amateur League before signing for Accrington Stanley in 1937. He had made 31 League appearances for the Peel Park club when Wolves paid £400 for his services in March 1929. He missed very few games over the next four seasons and was ever-present in 1931–32 when the club won the Second Division Championship. He had appeared in 143 first-team games for the

Molineux club when he was transferred to Fulham in November 1932. Tootill's last match for Wolves was against Arsenal at Molineux, when he conceded seven goals. He made his début for the Cottagers in a 2–1 win at Charlton Athletic and over the next six seasons was the club's first-choice keeper. He was in outstanding form in the 1935–36 FA Cup run, which ended in the semi-finals against Sheffiled United; his saves in the goalless fifth-round tie at Chelsea were particularly memorable. Tootill went on to appear in 214 League and Cup games for Fulham before moving to Crystal Palace. He played regularly for the Selhurst Park club during the Second World War, appearing in 144 games before he announced his retirement in 1945.

TORRANCE, JIMMY Scotsman Jimmy Torrance played his early football with the Rob Roy and Ashfield clubs before coming south to play for Fulham. He made his début for the Cottagers as an inside-forward in a 2–0 defeat at Bolton Wanderers in September 1910. In his first three seasons with the club, he found his first-team opportunities limited due to the fine form of Herbert Pearce and Tim Coleman but, switching to wing-half towards the end of the 1913–14 season, he became a first-team regular. During the First World War, Torrance appeared in more games for the Cottagers than anyone -- 135. He continued to be a member of the Fulham side until 1926, when, after scoring 35 goals in 355 League and Cup games, he left Craven Cottage to become player-manager of Walsall. Torrance, who took trainer Jimmy Sharp with him, was in charge at Fellows Park for just two seasons and took the Saddlers to 18th in the Third Division (South) in 1927–28 before leaving the game.

TRANSFERS The club's record transfer fee received is £800,000 from Bristol City for Tony Thorpe in February 1998. The club's record transfer fee paid is £3 million to Sunderland for Lee Clark in September 1999.

TRAVERS, BARNEY Sunderland-born centre-forward Barney Travers began his Football League career with his home-town club in the first season of competitive football after the First World War. During that campaign of 1919–20, Travers was the Wearsiders' leading scorer, his total of 22 goals including hat-tricks against Notts County (home 3–1) and West Bromwich Albion (home 4–1). In February 1921, Travers left Roker Park to join Fulham for £3,000 fee, a record at the time. His first game for the Cottagers was in a 3–1 defeat at Barnsley and in the last

16 games of the season he top-scored with 11 goals. In 1921–22, Travers netted a hat-trick in a 6–0 home win over Hull City and had taken his tally of goals to 29 in 49 games when he was implicated in a bribery scandal after the crucial promotion match at South Shields which Fulham lost 1–0. Banned for life, Travers tried to make a comeback in Spanish football but, when the authorities in that country learned of the ban, he was prevented from playing there as well.

TURNER, HUGH Wigan-born goalkeeper Hugh Turner began his career with Darlington club Felling Colliery before signing for the town's Third Division (North) club in June 1924. After failing to make their League side, he joined Northern Alliance club, High Fell, from where he signed for Huddersfield Town in April 1926. Although he arrived at Leeds Road immediately after the Yorkshire club's triple Championship success and missed the 1928 FA Cup final through injury, he did play in the 1930 final which Town lost 2–0 to Arsenal. Between April 1928 and March 1932, Turner appeared in 181 consecutive League and Cup games but in June 1937, after 394 first-team games for Huddersfield, he left to join Fulham. Turner, who made two appearances for England, replacing the injured Harry Hibbs, made his Fulham début on the opening day of the 1937–38 season in a 4–0 defeat at Plymouth Argyle. Injuries forced him to share the goalkeeping duties that season with Alf Tootill but in 1938–39, Turner, who kept 13 clean sheets, was one of three ever-presents. He then played in three League South 'B' matches for the Craven Cottage club before retiring.

U

UNDEFEATED Fulham have never remained undefeated at home throughout a League season although they lost just one home game in seasons 1912–13, 1948–49 and 1998–99. The club's longest undefeated sequence in the Football League is of 15 matches between 26 January 1999 and 13 April 1999. Fulham's longest run of undefeated home matches is 28 between 22 January 1921 and 8 April 1922.

UNUSUAL GOALS Nick Cusack scored one of the most unusual goals of recent times in Fulham's 1–0 win over Scarborough at Craven Cottage on 13 January 1996. The Yorkshire side's keeper Ian Ironside made a dreadful hash of trying to keep a back-pass in play. He batted the ball high in the air, failed to grab it three times on the bounce and, finally, the Fulham player side-footed it into the net.

UTILITY PLAYERS A utility player is one of those particularly gifted footballers who can play in several different positions. After the mid-1960s, players were encouraged to become more adaptable. At the same time, however, much less attention came to be paid to the implication of wearing a certain numbered shirt and, accordingly, some of the more versatile players came to wear almost all the different numbered shirts at some stage or another, although this did not necessarily indicate a great variety of tactical duties. Stan Brown, who appeared in 397 League and Cup games for the Cottagers between 1961 and 1973, wore all ten different numbered outfield shirts during his time at Craven Cottage – being equally effective in defence, midfield or attack. Alan Slough wore all the different numbered shirts except five and nine during the 187 games he played for the Cottagers, although he is best remembered as a hard-working midfield player. Most recently, the versatile John Marshall appeared in every position except goalkeeper.

V

VICTORIES IN A SEASON – HIGHEST The highest number of wins in a season by the Craven Cottage club is 31, when they won the Second Division Championship in 1998–99.

VICTORIES IN A SEASON – LOWEST Fulham's poorest performance was in 1968–69 when they won only seven matches out of their 42 League games and finished bottom of the Second Division.

W

WALKER, WILLIE Durham-born winger Willie Walker played all his early football in and around Darlington for a number of clubs before joining Fulham from Darlington St Augustine in September 1909. He made his début the following month in a 1–1 draw at Blackpool, going on to score four goals in 17 games that season. That campaign also saw him win a London Challenge Cup winners' medal before he won a regular place in the Fulham side in 1910–11. Walker missed very few games in the seasons up to the outbreak of the First World War, creating numerous goalscoring opportunities for the likes of Herbert Pearce and Tim Coleman. However, he scored a fair share himself, netting ten in 32 games in 1912–13 as Fulham finished ninth in Division Two. On 15 February 1913, Walker became the first Fulham player to be sent off in a League match, receiving his marching orders in a 3–2 win at Bradford. He was still the club's first-choice left-winger when League football resumed in 1919 but in the summer of 1921, after scoring 26 goals in 176 League and Cup games, he left Craven Cottage to end his career with Lincoln City.

WAR Fulham lost a number of players fighting for their country in the Second World War. Winger Dennis Higgins, who scored 12 goals in 32 games including a hat-trick against Bradford in January 1939, was killed in North Africa in 1942. Other players killed in action included former Fulham favourite Jimmy Temple and promising youngsters George Fairburn and Ernie Tuckett.

The most famous Fulham player to lose his life during the hostilities was wing-half Jimmy Tompkins. The Edmonton-born player, who appeared in 163 games, was a private in the Territorial Army when war broke out but by 1944 he had worked his way up to major. He was killed at Normandy in the D-Day landings

WARTIME FOOTBALL In spite of the outbreak of war in 1914, the major football Leagues embarked upon their planned programme of matches for the ensuing season and these were completed on schedule at the end of April the following year. The season saw Fulham finish twelfth in Division Two. The club then joined the London Combination but it was only in the last two wartime seasons that there was any real structure to the competition. The Cottagers' best performance came in 1917–18 when they finished third out of ten clubs, behind Spurs and Chelsea. Aided by a number of illustrious 'guest' players, Fulham reached the final of the London Victory Cup but lost 3–0 to Chelsea in front of a 36,000 crowd at Highbury. In contrast to the events of 1914, when war was declared on 3 September 1939 the Football League programme of 1939–40 was immediately suspended and the government forbade any major sporting events – there was no football of any description until October. In the three League matches that had been played, between the end of August and the declaration of war, Fulham drew with Luton Town (home 1–1) but lost to Bury (away 1–3) and West Ham United (away 1–2). Fulham later joined the League South 'B' and in 1939–40 finished fifth out of ten clubs. The following season, the ten Leagues were grouped into two regional sections, Northern and Southern. League placings were worked out on goal average and Fulham were judged to have finished 23rd out of 34 clubs. In 1941–42, the Cottagers joined the breakaway London League and finished 11th out of 16 clubs. For the remaining seasons of wartime football, the club competed in the League's Southern Section but had their best campaign immediately after the war when a 42–match season was restored in 1945–46 and they finished eighth. In the various cup competitions played during the war, the club's best performance came in 1939–40 when they reached the semi-final of the League Cup only to lose 4–3 to West Ham United, the eventual winners. Ronnie Rooke dominated the club's goalscoring during this period, scoring a remarkable 212 goals in 199 games and being rewarded with an appearance for England against Wales in 1942.

WATNEY CUP The Watney Cup was Britain's first commercially sponsored tournament, a pre-season competition for the top two highest-scoring teams in each division of the Football League the previous season. Only clubs with no European involvement could compete. In the club's only match in the competition on 1 August 1970, Fulham entertained Derby County but, despite two goals from Vic Halom, they lost 5–3 to the Rams after extra-time.

WEATHER CONDITIONS On Saturday 1 September 1906, Fulham played their opening game of their last-ever season of Southern League football against Norwich City at Carrow Road on what is thought to be the hottest day the League programme has ever been contested. The temperature reached above 90F (32C). The Cottagers played out a goalless draw.

WEBSTER, MALCOLM Goalkeeper Malcolm Webster represented Doncaster and England Schoolboys before joining Arsenal as an apprentice in May 1966. Having won two England Youth caps, he made three League appearances in the Gunners' side in the first half of the 1969–70 season, making his début in the London derby against Spurs at Highbury in a match which Arsenal lost 3–2. Soon afterwards, Geoff Barnett joined the Gunners from Everton as understudy to Bob Wilson and Webster left Highbury for Fulham. His first game for the Cottagers was in December 1969 when Fulham beat Bristol Rovers 3–1. He kept his place for the rest of the season and the club finished fourth in Division Three. The following season he helped the club win promotion to the Second Division, keeping 16 clean sheets in 35 games. After losing his place to Peter Mellor, Webster, who had made 104 appearances, joined Southend United and later Cambridge United. Whilst at the Abbey Stadium he won a Fourth Division Championship winners' medal in 1976–77 and then helped the Us win promotion to Division Two the following season. After a career that spanned over 500 first-class matches, he became coach at Cambridge and later started up his own goalkeeping schools as well as coaching aspiring keepers at various League clubs.

WHITE, WALTER Scottish international Walter White was born in Hurlford in May 1882 and began his career with local clubs, Britannia, Portland Thistle and Kilmarnock. In May 1902, Bolton Wanderers signed him from Hurlford Thistle and he soon established himself in the Trotters' side. Having played for the Wanderers in the 1904 FA Cup final, White came to prominence the following season when his 24 goals helped Bolton win promotion to the First Division. His haul included three hat-tricks in the wins over Grimsby Town (home 4–1), Burton United (home 7–1) and Doncaster Rovers (away 4–0). His goalscoring exploits continued in the top-flight and in April 1907, he won the first of two Scottish caps when he played against England at St James Park. After the Wanderers had suffered relegation in 1907–08, White, who had scored 93 goals in 217 games, left to play for Everton. He made 43 League appearances and scored ten goals for the Goodison club, helping them to runners-up spot in the League in 1908–09 and to the FA Cup semi-finals the following season. In October 1910 he joined Fulham, making his début in a 1–0 win at Gainsborough Trinity. In the years leading up to the outbreak of the First World War, White was a virtual ever-present in the Fulham side, though the Cottagers converted him from inside-forward to wing-half. After the hostilities, his first-team opportunities were limited and he made the last of 203 appearances in a 1–0 win at Bury in February 1923 at the age of 40 years 275 days.

WILKINS, RAY Ray Wilkins began his career with Chelsea where he became a great crowd favourite in his six seasons with the Stamford Bridge club for his aggressive midfield play and spectacular goals. He captained his team to promotion to Division One in 1976–77 but was unable to stop Chelsea's slide back to Division Two in 1978–79. By then a regular choice for England, Wilkins moved to Manchester United in the summer of 1979 for a fee of £825,000. He spent five good years at Old Trafford and United came close to winning the League Championship in his first season. He won an FA Cup winners' medal in 1983 but in 1984 joined the exodus to Italy, signing for AC Milan for £1.5 million. After three years, he lost his place and moved to French club Paris St Germain. However, Wilkins hardly got a game in the French team and was rescued by Graeme Souness who signed him for Glasgow Rangers in 1987. He missed barely a game in two years at Ibrox Park, winning Scottish League Championship and Skol Cup winners' medals. In November 1989 he returned to London to play for Queen's Park Rangers and did not miss a game in his first two seasons at the club. Awarded an OBE in the honours list, he went on to play in 182 games for the Loftus Road club before joining Crystal Palace. He made just one appearance for the Eagles before he broke a foot. Awarded an MBE in 1994, he rejoined Queen's Park Rangers as player-manager, a position he held for two years. After just eight

Ray Wilkins

games of the 1997–98 season, Fulham manager Micky Adams was dismissed and, amid much publicity, Kevin Keegan arrived with Ray Wilkins as team manager. Fulham made the play-offs despite losing their last three games, but that poor form cost Wilkins his job. He is now back at Chelsea as coach.

WILSON, ROBERT Robert Wilson joined Fulham as an associate schoolboy, signing apprentice forms in July 1977 and turning professional just under two years later. When he arrived at Craven Cottage, Wilson was a full-back but was later converted into a midfield player. He made his début in a 1–1 draw at Blackburn Rovers in a third-round FA Cup match in January 1980, following it with his first Football League appearance four days later, also in Lancashire as the Cottagers lost 3–2 to Preston North End. He started the following campaign in the first-team and held his place in the side for the next five seasons, helping Fulham win promotion to the Second Division in 1981–82. Wilson found the net on 37 occasions in his 200 League and Cup outings, many of them vital goals, before moving to Millwall for £57,000 in August 1985. After ending his only season at the Den as the Lions' leading scorer, with 12 goals, he joined Luton Town but, after only 24 appearances, rejoined the Cottagers. He had taken his tally of goals to 41 in 251 games when he left Fulham a second time to play for Huddersfield Town. The much-travelled midfielder joined his fifth League club, Rotherham United, in September 1991, and ended his career with the Millers.

WOODWARD, VIV A Welsh Schoolboy international, Viv Woodward played his early football in the Welsh League before moving to play non-League football for Folkestone. His performances for the Kent club led to Fulham offering him professional terms in January 1936. He made his début for the Cottagers two months later in a 5–2 defeat at Leicester City but it was midway through the 1936–37 season before he established himself in the Fulham side. Able to play in all the forward positions, he struck up a good understanding with Ronnie Rooke and, in 1937–38, netted 15 goals in 33 games. During the Second World War, Woodward scored 41 goals in 90 games for Fulham including a hat-trick in the 7–5 defeat at the hands of Charlton Athletic in April 1940. His performances during the hostilities led to his representing Wales in a wartime international and though he was still a member of the Fulham side when League football resumed in 1946–47, he had lost his best years to the war. He had scored 24 goals in 95 League and Cup games when, in February 1950, he left to play for Millwall, retiring the following year.

WORRALL, TED A cousin of the legendary goalkeeper Sam Hardy, full-back Ted Worrall played his early football for Sheffield Wednesday, making 103 League appearances for the Owls before the outbreak of the First World War. After the end of hostilities, he came south to look for work and was given a free transfer by Wednesday so that he could join Fulham. He made his début for the Cottagers in a 2–1 home defeat by West Ham United in November 1919, after which he established himself as a first-team regular. Forming a good full-back partnership with Alec Chaplin, he went on to appear in 96 League and Cup games before losing his place to Tom Fleming. Worrall left Craven Cottage in the summer of 1922 to play for Aberdare Athletic before later joining New Brighton. An ever-present in each of his two seasons with the Wirral club, Ted Worrall ended his League career with Southport.

WORSLEY, BERT The speedy winger began his career with Altrincham and spent some time on Bolton Wanderers' books before playing for Cheshire League side, Manchester North End. His impressive performances over the next three seasons led to Leeds United securing his services in August 1932. He was unlucky enough to make his début in the worst defeat in United's history as the Yorkshire side went down 8–1 at Stoke City in August 1934. He had made only three appearances for the Elland Road club when he joined Fulham in the summer of 1935. After making his début for the Cottagers in a 1–1 home draw against Norwich City, he went on to become an important member of the side that reached that season's FA Cup semi-final, scoring one of Fulham's goals in a 2–1 third-round win over Brighton and Hove Albion. That season, his best for the club, he netted ten goals in 33 League and Cup games. A crop of injuries kept him out of the side, however, and he retired prematurely: he had scored 17 goals in 112 games. Ironically, he did come back to play for Fulham, at Derby County in August 1945, when the Cottagers were critically depleted by injury.

WORST STARTS The club's worst-ever start to a season was in 1937–38, mirrored by 1953–54. On both occasions they went ten League games before recording the first victory of the season. In 1937–38, the Cottagers drew five and lost five of the opening fixtures before beating Tottenham Hotspur 3–1. In 1953–54, Fulham drew four and lost six games before ending the famine with a 3–1 win over Nottingham Forest.

X

'X' In football, 'x' traditionally stands for a draw. The club record for the number of draws in a season is 17, in 1986–87, 1992–93 and 1995–96.

XMAS DAY Christmas Day was once a regular date in the footballing calendar but the game's authorities dropped the fixture in the late 1950s. Fulham first played on Christmas Day in 1908 when they were held to a goalless draw at home by Chesterfield. Their first win on Christmas Day came the following year when they beat Hull City, also at Craven Cottage, 3–1. On Christmas Day 1929, the Cottagers beat Bristol Rovers 6–2 and Bill Haley became the first Fulham player to score a hat-trick in this fixture. In 1930, Fulham lost 4–1 at Swindon Town, their heaviest Christmas Day defeat, but gained revenge on Boxing Day, beating the Robins 6–1. In 1953, when Fulham beat Plymouth Argyle 3–1, Bedford Jezzard scored all the club's goals to become the second Fulham player to net a hat-trick on Christmas Day. The club last played a League match on Christmas Day in 1957 when a goal by Roy Dwight helped them beat Lincoln City 1–0 at Sincil Bank.

Y

YOUNGEST PLAYER The youngest player ever to appear in a first-class fixture for Fulham, Tony Mahoney, was 17 years 38 days old when he played in the Second Division match against Cardiff City (home 1–2) on 6 November 1976.

Z

ZENITH Though Fulham reached the 1975 FA Cup final as a Second Division club, the Cottagers have enjoyed their best period in the Football League in recent years. After winning promotion from the Third Division in 1996–97 and reaching the play-offs the following season, Fulham took the First Division by storm in 1998–99, winning the Championship with 101 points, 14 clear of runners-up Walsall. During the course of that memorable season, Fulham were unbeaten in 15 matches between 26 January 1999 and 13 April 1999.